ANCIENT DELHI

For Madhav and Raghav

ANCIENT DELHI

Second Edition

Upinder Singh

OXFORD

UNIVERSITY PRESS

OXFORD
UNIVERSITY PRESS

Oxford University Press is a department of the University of Oxford.
It furthers the University's objective of excellence in research, scholarship,
and education by publishing worldwide. Oxford is a registered trademark of
Oxford University Press in the UK and in certain other countries

Published in India by
Oxford University Press
22 Workspace, 2nd Floor, 1/22 Asaf Ali Road, New Delhi 110002

First Edition published in 1999
Oxford India Paperbacks (Second edition) 2006
28th impression 2026

ISBN-13: 978-0-19-568405-6
ISBN-10: 0-19-568405-2

Typeset in Baskerville
Printed in India by Saurabh Printers Pvt. Ltd., Noida, UP

Preface to the Second Edition

About eight years ago, while I was teaching in St. Stephen's College, my former teacher Muhammad Amin asked me if I would write a book on Delhi's ancient history. It was Lalit Sharma's idea. Lalit was Chairman and Managing Director of the Delhi Tourism and Transport Development Corporation in 1996–7. Holding the radical view that the Delhi government should aim at something more cerebral than setting up musical fountains (which were then the rage), he decided to commission a series of monographs on various aspects of Delhi's history and culture. The monographs would be scholarly yet lively and interesting, aimed at general readers, not academics.

My first reaction was to refuse. I was at that time submerged in the routines of home (my sons were small and a handful) and work. Also, ancient Delhi did not fall within the purview of my research interests. I was not sure whether I wanted to write a book for the Delhi Tourism and Transport Development Corporation. It did not sound particularly prestigious, although I was assured that various high-flying publishing houses would be approached to publish the series. Gradually my hesitation melted and I decided that it was worth a shot.

When I started looking for material on the ancient history of Delhi, I realized that there was really very little primary source material or secondary literature in the form of books or articles on the subject. The available histories of Delhi spoke about medieval and modern times and had practically nothing to say about the ancient period. This made my task simultaneously easy as well as difficult. It was easy, because I did not have to spend months or years researching the subject—there simply wasn't that much material to go through. But given this fact, how was I to construct a meaningful and connected narrative? I decided to collect every single piece of evidence I could lay my hands on—from texts, inscriptions, archaeological data, documented local traditions etc. I then framed my data within a larger narrative of the history of the Indian subcontinent.

One of the things I realized at an early stage was that I could use some of the information and insights I had gained while doing an archaeological field survey in 1994–5 in Ballabgarh along with Nayanjot Lahiri and Tarika Uberoi. This village-to-village survey proved to be an important part of my intellectual development as a historian, because it brought me face to face both with the tangible past and the past as it lingers in the lives and memories of present-day communities.

The most difficult part about writing the book was the stylistic requirement. I had to very self-consciously shake myself loose from the conventions of academic writing. Concepts and technical terms had to be explained in a simple and straightforward manner. Footnotes were to be kept to a minimum. This was a real learning experience. Since then, I have become more and more convinced that it is possible, in fact necessary, to combine scholarship with readability and that one of the measures of good history writing is that anybody should be able to read, comprehend, and enjoy it.

Shortly after I had handed over my typescript, Lalit Sharma moved on to a new assignment in the Andaman Islands and his successor in Delhi Tourism was not particularly interested in the monograph project. Neither was there a pile of monographs waiting to be published because the other authors who had been commissioned to write them had not taken the deadline as literally as I had. Once it was clear that the Delhi government had no interest in my book, I approached Oxford University Press, who took it on.

That was in 1999. Since then, some new data on the ancient history of the Delhi area has surfaced and there are some details that needed to be added to my narrative. But more significantly, my own understanding of the issues I discussed in my book has grown. Hence this new edition. Recently, the University of Delhi has introduced a new course on Delhi's history. At last, university students will be exposed to the immediacy of history as it exists all around us. I am convinced that it is the percolation and spread of this sort of interest—of young students and Dilli-*wallah*s of all ages and backgrounds—that will stimulate new discoveries and enrich our understanding of Delhi's ancient past.

It will also create the awareness which is necessary for the conservation of Delhi's rich historical heritage to become a concern shared by people who live in this city.

I need to add a few more acknowledgements to this new edition of *Ancient Delhi*. I would like to thank Sunil Kumar for several valuable suggestions regarding the early medieval history of Delhi, B.S.R. Babu for information on the site of Jhatikara, and Anand Taneja for sharing his research on the living history of Firoz Shah Kotla and the Pir Ghaib.

Upinder Singh

Acknowledgements
to the First Edition

I would like to thank

Mr. Lalit Sharma and Mr. Mohammad Amin, for the idea and project out of which this book emerged

Mr. P.S. Dwivedi for reading through the manuscript thoroughly and making valuable comments and corrections

Mr. T.K. Roy for making the maps

Aditya Arya and Ravi Agarwal for photographs

Nayanjot Lahiri for the shared experience of field-work in the Faridabad area and general moral support

and Vijay Tankha for somewhat erratic but useful stylistic advice.

I would also like to thank the Archaeological Survey of India and the National Museum, New Delhi for permission to use in this book some of the photographs from their collections.

I owe special thanks to Dr. B.S.R. Babu, Deputy Director, Department of Archaeology, Government of Delhi, for making available to me photographs of the exciting discoveries at Bhorgarh and Mandoli.

Contents

List of Illustrations

List of colour plates

(between pp. 56–7)

The Bahapur rocks
Photograph: Author

The Delhi-Topra pillar
Photograph: V. Tankha

The Delhi-Meerut pillar
Photograph: V. Tankha

(between pp. 64–5)

The ascent of the Tilpat mound
Photograph: N. Lahiri

Village shrine; Tilpat
Photograph: N. Lahiri

Nachauli: section of the mound
Photograph: N. Lahiri

Ancient Shiva *linga* in the midst of fields; Nachauli
Photograph: N. Lahiri

(between pp. 80–1)

The Mehrauli iron pillar
Photograph: Aditya Arya

Pillars of the Qutb mosque
Photograph: Aditya Arya

(between pp. 96–7)

Painting of Prithviraja Chauhan with poet Chand Bardai;
 Jodhpur style
Courtesy: National Museum

The Suraj Kund reservoir
Photograph: Aditya Arya

The dam at Anangpur
Photograph: Aditya Arya

Maps

Introduction to the Second Edition

The clues to Delhi's ancient past survive in the form of a few explored or excavated sites, stray artefacts, legends, and local traditions.[1] Seemingly nondescript villages lie on top of ancient mounds, where broken pieces of ancient pottery can be seen on the surface or studded in exposed sections. Old and broken sculptures are sometimes assembled and worshipped in village shrines. Ancient remains can also sometimes be seen at popular picnic spots (the reservoir at Suraj Kund), in the midst of agricultural fields (the Shiva linga in Nachauli village), in people's courtyards (the Tilpat cross-bar), in remote shrines (the Gothra-Mohabbatabad Shiva linga) and as prized possessions of villagers (the Vishnu sculpture at Chirsi).[2]

The meagre and scattered evidence may be a reason why the earliest history of this area has generated less interest than its medieval and modern past. Delhi has a rather dismal representation in ancient texts, except for its possible connection with Indraprastha of the *Mahabharata* legend. As for archaeological evidence, the large monumental structures associated with medieval and modern elites—palaces, mosques, and

---

[1] I am using the term 'ancient' in a very loose sense here. This book covers many different segments of the past including the prehistoric, protohistoric, early historical, and early medieval. In the Indian context, historians generally use the term 'early medieval' to refer to the period between the sixth and twelfth/thirteenth centuries AD.

[2] All these instances are discussed in the book.

imperial edifices of the colonial era—have overshadowed the ancient stone tools, terracottas, and broken pieces of pottery, relics of the everyday lives of ordinary people. The comparative lack of interest in Delhi's ancient past may perhaps be the result of a greater interest in things that are closer to contemporary experience and memory. While these factors may be responsible for the lack of popular enthusiasm, for historians, they simply translate into a greater challenge. This includes intensifying the search for new evidence. It also involves creating and furthering a sensitivity towards the extraordinary nature of apparently ordinary artefacts, animating them by connecting them with the people who made and used them and with their times.

The Contributions of Nineteenth Century Archaeologists and Scholars

Discoverers are as important as discoveries. Among the early attempts to document the ancient and medieval remains in the Delhi area, the contribution of certain men has to be highlighted. One of them is Syed Ahmed Khan. Best known as a socio-religious reformer of nineteenth century India, he is significant for us as the author of a monumental Urdu work *Asar-al-Sanadid* (The Legacy of Heroes). The book, illustrated with sketches made by Mirza Shah Rukh Beg, was published in 1846 and a second revised edition appeared in 1854. It opened with a Persian couplet, 'The ruins of old buildings faithfully tell the story of the kings of bygone ages.' The book was the first detailed account of the monuments of Delhi, based on a careful analysis of a variety of literary sources as well as the author's own personal observations.

Although *Asar-al-Sanadid* emphasized the medieval structures of the Sultanate and Mughal periods, it also described ancient remains such as the iron pillar, Ashokan pillars, Anangpur dam, Anang Tal, and Suraj Kund. The second edition had a list of the dynasties of Delhi, including the Tomaras and Chauhans. It also included a chronological table of the fortresses and cities of Delhi, starting with Indraprastha, described as founded by Yudhishthira in *c*. 1450 BC and Delhi founded by King Dhuloo in 328 BC. An important aspect of the book was that it carried copies of inscriptions, including those on the Ashokan and Gupta pillars. Khan suggested that the Mehrauli iron pillar was originally made in the nineth century BC during the reign of a king named Medhava or Dhava, nineteenth in the line of descent after Yudhishthira. He thought that its Sanskrit inscription contained a posthumous record of the achievements of that king, possibly engraved in the third or fourth century AD.[3]

Two other names that stand out among the explorers who made a major contribution towards the documentation of Delhi's ancient and medieval remains are Alexander Cunningham and J.D.M. Beglar.[4] Cunningham was a Scotsman who arrived in Calcutta in 1833 and took up a job with the Bengal Engineers. For many years, he combined his duties as a military engineer with a pursuit of his interest in archaeology, numismatics, epigraphy, and history. Between 1861 and 1866, he worked as archaeological surveyor for the British Government of India. When the Archaeological Survey of India was established in 1871, Cunningham was chosen as director-general, a post he held till 1885.

As archaeological surveyor and director-general of the Archaeological Survey, Cunningham scoured town and countryside, searching out and documenting the archaeological remains of many parts of northern and central India. Delhi was part of his itinerary during his tour in the winter of 1862–3. In his report of this tour,[5] Cunningham described the medieval remains of the city, but his documentation of

[3] R. Nath, *Monuments of Delhi: Historical Study* (New Delhi, Ambika Publications, 1979), p. 79.

[4] I became interested in these archaeologists after writing *Ancient Delhi*. The results of my research are contained in my recent book *The Discovery of Ancient India: Early Archaeologists and the Beginnings of Archaeology* (New Delhi, Permanent Black, 2004).

[5] Alexander Cunningham, *Four Reports Made during the Years 1862–63–64–65*, Archaeological Survey Reports, vol. 2 (Simla, 1871).

ancient remains (he called them 'Hindu') on the basis of texts, monuments, and oral and written literature, was the first of its kind.

Cunningham described the three ancient pillars in Delhi—the two
stone pillars of Ashoka and the Gupta period iron pillar in Mehrauli—
and discussed the text of their inscriptions. He narrated the history of
these pillars in medieval and modern times. He identified and mapped
the circuit of the walls and gates of the early medieval forts of Lal Kot
and Qila Rai Pithora. He collected various local traditions connected
with Delhi in the epics, Puranas, Rajput legends, Persian chronicles,
and the accounts of traditional genealogists. He proposed the plausible
identification of Ptolemy's Indapat with Indraprastha and the unlikely
identification of his Daiddala with Dilli.

Cunningham's archaeological survey of Delhi was followed a few
years later by a similar survey by J.D.M. Beglar, an Armenian settled
in Bengal. Employed as an engineer with the Public Works Department,
he devoted himself to a study of historical monuments and photography
in his free time. In 1871, he was appointed Cunningham's assistant in
the Archaeological Survey of India. The survey of Delhi was Beglar's
first assignment.[6] His main focus was on the Mehrauli area, especially
Lal Kot and the Qutb complex. Beglar made a number of wild specula-
tions, arguing for instance that the Qutb minar was originally a Hindu
monument (Syed Ahmed Khan had suggested this many years earlier).
Even more off the mark was his hypothesis that the Qutb mosque
went through three successive stages, first as a Buddhist structure, then
a Hindu one, and finally a Muslim one. Beglar's bumblings and errors
should not surprise us, as he was an amateur who was learning archaeology on the job.

In spite of being a novice, Beglar's documentation of Lal Kot
was fairly sound. He described the tank known as the Anang Tal and

---

[6] Its results were published in J.D.M. Beglar and A.C.L. Carlleyle, *Report for the Year
1871–72, Delhi, Agra,* Archaeological Survey Reports, vol. 4 (Calcutta, 1874).

discovered a new gateway in the western part of the fortification wall. He traced the walls of Lal Kot and Qila Rai Pithora. Disagreeing with Cunningham, he gave detailed evidence and arguments to prove that Lal Kot represented two different structural phases—the western part the original Rajput fort of Anangapala and the eastern part the enlargement made during the time of Ala-ud-din Khilji. Beglar excavated several sections of the Lal Kot walls, analysed the proportion of lime at different points, and identified the different structural phases. His general point about two structural phases in the building of Lal Kot—one belonging to the Rajput, the other to the Sultanate phase—was confirmed by the more extensive and systematic excavations conducted at the site many decades later. The map Beglar drew of the circuit of Lal Kot continues to be reproduced in recent writings.

In more recent years, our understanding of the ancient history of the Delhi area has gradually increased as a result of the explorations and excavations by archaeologists of the Delhi circle of the Archaeological Survey of India, the Archaeological Department of the Delhi government, and university scholars and researchers. Nevertheless, there are still many gaps in the story. This is due to inadequate investigations and the non-publication of the results of certain crucial investigations. Many decades down the line, there is still no detailed report of the Purana Qila excavations.[7] In the absense of such a report, the details of the valuable discoveries made in the excavations at this important site remain a secret to which only the excavators are privy.

[7] The Archaeological Survey of India no doubt has onerous responsibilities and many achievements to its credit. But its record of publishing the results of its excavations makes dismal reading. Consider the following estimates collated by Dilip K. Chakrabarti in his *Archaeology in the Third World: A History of Indian Archaeology Since 1947* (New Delhi, D.K. Printworld, 2003):

Period	1963–5	1965–73	1973–83	1983–90	1990–5
Number of sites excavated	144	112	191	145	106
Number of reports published	39	19	46	14	12

New data

Not much new data on Delhi's ancient and early medieval history has
emerged since the first edition of *Ancient Delhi*, and not all of it has been
published. As far as prehistoric sites are concerned, the excavations at
Anangpur remain the only large-scale ones conducted so far. Very little
has been done to intensively investigate the sites listed in the preliminary
survey conducted by Chakrabarti and Lahiri[8] many years ago or to
extend such investigations to other areas. One of the notable exceptions
is the discovery of palaeoliths and microliths on the campus of the
Jawaharlal Nehru University by Mudit Trivedi and his attempts to
analyse them within their geomorphological context. Among the other
interesting remains documented by Trivedi in his research area are a
semicircular alignment of stones and rock bruisings.[9] This study shows
how important additions to the knowledge of Delhi's prehistory do
not necessarily depend on large-scale excavations conducted by official
agencies, and that a great deal can be achieved through a thorough
surface investigation even by a single individual. Prehistoric stone tools
will only be found if people look for them and many more stone age
sites are waiting to be discovered and studied. We should also be
aware of the fact that quarrying in the Badarpur hills is destroying
valuable evidence of the prehistory of the Delhi region.

In 1996, a team of archaeologists of the Department of Archaeology
of the Delhi government led by B.S.R. Babu conducted a small-scale
excavation at Jhatikara, a site located some 12 km south of Najafgarh.[10]
The mound here seems to have been spread over 3 acres, by now
mostly levelled and converted into agricultural fields. The uppermost

---

[8] D.K. Chakrabarti and N. Lahiri, 'A Preliminary Report on the Stone Age of the Union
Territory of Delhi and Haryana,' *Man and Environment*, XI (1987), pp. 100–16.

[9] Mudit Trivedi, 'The Archaeology of Delhi: Perspectives from a survey of the Jawaharlal
Nehru University Campus', unpublished paper presented at the Manana (Devahuti-
Damodar Trust) seminar on Ancient India—New Research, Delhi, August 2005.

[10] The following information is based on personal communication from B.S.R. Babu. The
results of the Jhatikara excavations are likely to be published shortly.

section of the deposit was quite disturbed, the lower parts intact. The excavation revealed several phases of mud brick structures. These included a room with a hearth made of baked clay, a vase in a pit, a saddle quern (used for grinding food) and some miniature pots. This seems to have been a kitchen belonging to the early centuries AD. A large number of potsherds, mostly wheel-made, were unearthed in the excavations. The most common vessel was a bowl with a slightly incurved rim and heavy base. Fragments of vases of different sizes including ones with spouts, a basin with a sturdy rim, and carinated *handis* were also found. Some pieces of blue porcelain, glazed pottery with a sandy core, and a grey ware with incised designs were also found. The other discoveries included seven copper coins which are still being studied, two copper ear ornaments, one copper ring, a hoard of 82 terracotta beads, glass bangles, an animal figurine, and several iron nails.

The 1994–5 volume of *Indian Archaeology: A Review* reported the discovery of two fragmentary inscribed stone slabs, probably belonging to a single inscription. The specific place or context where they were found is not mentioned. The language of the inscriptions is Sanskrit and the letters belong to the Siddhamatrika script of the eighth or nineth century AD. The first inscription refers to the installation of a deity (whose name is lost) by a ruler who described as *Maharajadhiraja* (great king of kings) Sri Madhava. The second mentions two people named Bhatta Divakara and a *kayastha* (scribe) named Sajjana and makes intriguing references to the drawing of pictures (*chitra-rachana*), including those of kings.

As mentioned above, the Purana Qila report is still unpublished. However, a point of detail can be noted in relation to some of the male terracotta figurines found at this site.[11] Similar terracottas were

---

[11] These are depicted on p. 100 of this book.

found in the Lal Kot excavations in early Sultanate period levels. In view of this, the Purana Qila specimens should perhaps also be assigned to the early Sultanate and not to the Rajput period.

Among the discoveries at Lal Kot, the results of the analysis of the bone remains are interesting.[12] Levels associated with the Rajput period give evidence of goats and sheep (*Capra/ovis*) killed for food. Out of the 42 bone samples analysed, 41 belonged to these species, while one fragment represented a buffalo (*Bubalus bubalis*). In contrast, the bone fragments of the early Sultanate phase reveal a greater variety of animals and birds including goat, sheep, cattle, buffalo, deer, tortoise, and chicken.

Another important piece of evidence concerns the location of one or more mints in the Delhi area during the Rajput period. A number of Rajput billon coins with the bull motif on the obverse and a rider on a horse on the reverse have been found in various places. They some-times have additional symbols such as the trident and generally bear the name of the issuing king. P.C. Roy argued that these bull-and-horseman coins were probably minted in Delhi.[13] Texts of the early Sultanate phase in fact refer to such coins as 'Dilliwala' or 'Dhillika'.

John S. Deyell confirmed Roy's theory on the basis of various his-torical references and through an analysis of the fabric and metrology of the bull-and-horseman coins.[14] It is clear that a billon coinage made of silver and copper was minted in Delhi during the Tomara and Chauhan periods. These coins were of a uniform weight standard, and the surviving specimens have a mean weight of 3.38 g. The names that appear, on the coins are those of Tomara kings Sallakshanapala, Anangapala, Madanapala, and the Chauhan kings Pithimva (Prithviraja II),

[12] B.R. Mani. *Delhi: Threshold of the Orient: Studies in Archaeological Excavations* (N. Delhi, Aryan Books International, 1977), p. 77.

[13] P.C. Roy, 'Madanapala: The Issuer of the Horseman and Bull Type'. *Journal of the Numismatic Society of India*, 31 (1969), pp. 48–56; 'Notes on Some Medieval Coins', *Journal of the Numismatic Society of India*, 32 (1971), pp. 176–82.

[14] John S. Deyell, *Living Without Silver: The Monetary History of Early Medieval North India* (New Delhi, Oxford University Press, 1990), pp. 155, 179–80.

Somesvara, Chahada (Chahar), and Prithviraja (Prithviraja III). The names of all these kings have the honorific suffix 'Deva'. Hoards of the bull-and-horseman coins have been found outside the Tomara and Chauhan principalities as well, in the area north-west of Delhi and in the Punjab, and these coins continued to circulate for some time during the early Sultanate period.

Ancient mounds can lull us into a vision of a long, seamless past, stretching back endlessly, with one stage of material culture smoothly succeeding the other. But the fact that a certain site may have been occupied over many centuries does not necessarily mean that there was a continuity in the communities who lived there. Disruptions, movements, and migrations are a part of settlement history. For instance, the Jats and Meos are supposed to have moved into the Punjab area in the wake of the Arab conquest of Sind. Meo settlements are known in the upper doab region around Meerut by the twelfth century. The Meos lost their lands to Rajputs groups such as the Tomaras, Dors, Bargujars, and Chauhans. Subsequently, the Turkish and Afghan rulers pushed them out of Delhi, south-west into the Aravalli valleys.[15] Unfortunately. histories of the cultural and ethnic aspects of Delhi's communities are difficult to reconstruct for earlier times.

Landscapes and Settlements: The Importance of Micro-Studies
In reconstructing the history of an area, new evidence is no doubt important. But equally important are the perspectives from which we view the existing evidence. It is useful to contextualize the history of a particular area within the larger framework of the history of the subcontinent. But it is even more essential to understand its history in relation to its physical environment and as part of larger networks of human settlements, activities, and interactions.

[15] Shail Mayaram, *Resisting Regimes: Myth, Memory and the Shaping of a Muslim Identity* (New Delhi, Oxford University Press, 1997).

Ancient Delhi

The ancient landscape can be inferred in various ways such as from observation, geomorphological studies, evidence of flora and fauna, satellite imagery, and textual references. Many years ago, several old channels of the Yamuna river were identified by Grover and Bakliwal using Landsat imagery produced by remote sensing techniques. However, there is still a great deal that we do not know about the physical geography of the Delhi region in ancient times.

The intimate relationship between people, settlements, and their specific physical environment emerges most clearly in a micro-study. Take the example of our field survey of the Ballabgarh tehsil.[16] This village-to-village survey in Ballabgarh covered about 132 villages and led to the discovery of over 50 new sites, ranging from the protohistoric to the late medieval (the survey did not include stone age sites). The Ballabgarh micro-region consists of distinct ecological and socio-cultural zones and we classified our sites according to their location in the Yamuna riverine tract, the higher plains, and the Aravalli hills. The cataloguing of data included the location, size, and condition of the site, artefacts (including pottery and sculptures), and structural remains. We found traces of protohistoric habitation in the riverine plains and the higher plains. Between about the first and fifth/sixth centuries AD, settlements were spread through all three ecological zones, including the Aravalli hills. A majority were located along the palaeo-channels (old courses) of the Yamuna and in the catchment area of non-perennial streams flowing out from the Badarpur hills. In the hills, shrines and cult spots also tended to be located along such streams.

The lifestyles of the people living in these different ecological niches must have been different, the emphasis on pastoralism in the hills contrasting with the basic reliance on agriculture in the plains. Nevertheless, these niches were neither self-sufficient nor isolated. The people of the

---

[16] Nayanjot Lahiri, Upinder Singh and Tarika Uberoi, 'Preliminary Field Report on the Archaeology of Faridabad: the Ballabgarh Tehsil', *Man and Environment*, 31 (1), 1996, pp. 32–57.

hills must have provided raw materials such as quartzite, crystal, mica, and slate to the plains-people, and the latter must have exchanged these for agricultural produce and craft items. The relationship between these communities was probably not only an economic one. Today groups such as Gujars, Meos, and Jats live in the hills as well as plains and shrines nestled in the Ballabgarh hills attract pilgrim traffic from afar.

The history of a place has to combine the references in literary sources, results of major excavations, and micro-studies based on an intensive, grass-roots approach towards historical investigation. If such an approach was extended to other parts of the Delhi region, we would have a more detailed and textured picture of its ancient history.

Ancient Trade Routes

The Delhi area had a close relationship with Rajasthan, and raw materials and people flowed in from this region over the centuries. From the early medieval period onwards, the Aravallis provided a base and a refuge to groups from Rajasthan such as the Rajputs, Meos, and Gujars. Political elites from Rajasthan such as the Tomaras and Chauhans extended their control over the Delhi area. Many of the *bhats* (traditional geneologists) in the Ballabgarh area trace their origin to Rajasthan. Pilgrims move to and fro between Rajasthan and the Ballabgarh area to visit shrines.

We can widen Delhi's circle of interaction even further by piecing together the literary and archaeological evidence of ancient trade routes. Agricultural produce and certain types of stone and minerals found in the Delhi area may have formed items of commercial exchange in ancient times. But what is more significant is the fact that Delhi is located in the watershed between the Indus and Ganga river systems, at the gateway to the Ganga plains. This gave settlements in this region a strategic commercial importance.

From the early historical period, texts speak of two great trans-
regional routes, a northern route called the *Uttarapatha* and a southern one known as the *Dakshinapatha*. The *Uttarapatha* was the major
trans-regional land-cum-river trade route of northern India, stretching
from the north-western part of the subcontinent, across the Indo-
Gangetic plains up to the port of Tamralipti on the Bay of Bengal.
This route had a northern and southern sector. The northern sector
ran through Lahore, Jullundar, Saharanpur, along the Ganga plains to
Bijnor, and then through Gorakhpur, towards Bihar and Bengal in the
east. The southern sector connected Lahore, Raiwind, Bhatinda, Delhi,
Hastinapur, Kanpur, Lucknow, Varanasi, and Allahabad and then
moved on towards Pataliputra and Rajagriha. Many feeder routes in-
tersected with the main arteries of the *Uttarapatha*. These included
feeder routes into Rajasthan (an area rich in various types of metals
and minerals), Sindh, and eastwards into Bengal and Orissa.[17] Although
these routes are generally referred to as 'trade routes', they were really
tried and tested routes of communication and travel, traversed not
only by traders but by many others including philosophers, religious
teachers, pilgrims, monks, students, and professionals.

These routes connected settlements in the Delhi area with other
ancient settlements of north India such as those of Mathura, Taxila,
Varanasi, Shravasti, and Kausambi. The networks of interaction did
not stop here. The *Uttarapatha* connected with routes leading into
central and southern India. The *Dakshinapatha* linked Pataliputra in
Bihar to Pratishthan on the Godavari. The routes connecting different
parts of the subcontinent tied up with land and maritime routes leading

---

[17] Nayanjot Lahiri, *The Archaeology of Indian Trade Routes Upto c. 200 BC: Resource Use, Resource Access and Lines of Communication* (New Delhi, Oxford University Press, 1992),
pp. 367–77. Lahiri has shown how archaeological evidence corroborates the literary references to the Uttarapatha. On the Uttarapatha, also see Moti Chandra, *Trade and Trade Routes
in Ancient India* (New Delhi, Abhinav Publications, 1977), pp. 12–22.

into areas outside the subcontinent such as Afghanistan, Central Asia, West Asia, East and south-east Asia, and Europe. Of course the history of these trade routes was a dynamic one, consisting of continuities as well as changes. These changes affected the fortunes of settlements that lay along their paths.

Epic Legends, Local Traditions, and History

An investigation into Delhi's ancient history can be expanded to include another important question—how is the landscape, especially the historical landscape, experienced and understood by people who live today in its midst? Villagers living in the Delhi area are aware of the changing course of the Yamuna over time in their classification of land into *khadar* (the new alluvium) and *bangar* (old alluvium). Mounds, referred to as *kheras* or *tilas*, are usually understood by inhabitants as evidence of their village being old, although they tend to be rather vague about just *how* old it might be ('very, very old' is the general refrain). Places where old pottery fragments are found are known but dimly understood. At the villages of Tilpat, Sihi, and Bisrakh, discussed in this book,[18] we have fascinating examples of ancient remains getting entwined with local and epic legends.

Local traditions—that is, beliefs current among the people of a locality—often intercede between historical or mythical event and historical memory, tying places to epic events and characters. It is in fact local tradition, the earliest records of which go back to the fourteenth century, that locate ancient Indraprastha, capital of the Pandava heroes of the *Mahabharata*, at the site of the Purana Qila in Delhi. How are the intangible, invisible memories and reworkings of the past reflected in ancient legends and local traditions to be interpreted from the historical point of view?

---

[18] See in chap. 4 of this book, section 'Tilpat, Sihi, and Bisrakh', pp. 39–43.

Epic legends and local traditions cannot be treated on par with history.[19] In some cases, the details are so fantastic that the issue of considering them as historical fact simply does not arise. But though the details of the stories may be clearly unhistorical, they may have been woven around certain events that actually happened. Or they may have historically significant sub-texts.

Public or scholarly interest in sites mentioned in the *Mahabharata* and *Ramayana* cannot in itself be considered illegitimate. However, the issue is one of priorities, of whether the direction of archaeological research should be steered or dominated by such an interest, of how much energy and resources should be invested in satisfying it, and whether the sorts of questions that people want to be answered can in fact be decisively answered by archaeology. Archaeology can tell us whether Hastinapura, Indraprastha, and Ayodhya were the sites of ancient settlements, but it cannot tell us for sure whether the *Mahabharata* war happened or where Rama was born. And when such investigations get entangled with larger political agendas, such as at Ayodhya, the issue of 'epic archaeology' no longer remains an exclusively academic issue.

Nineteenth-century archaeologists such as Cunningham and Beglar were not immune to the lure and mystique of the *Ramayana* and *Mahabharata* and tried to identify several places mentioned in the epics. But they were busier trying to identify places mentioned in Buddhist texts, Graeco-Roman accounts and the travellogues of the Chinese pilgrims Faxian and Xuanzang. This sort of approach led to major breakthroughs in historical geography and resulted in a mapping of a large number of ancient settlements. However, the casualty of this

---

[19] On the correlation of the Indian epics with archaeology, see Brajadulal Chattoadhyaya, 'Indian Archaeology and the Epic Traditions', in *Studying Early India: Archaeology, Texts, and Historical Issues* (New Delhi, Permanent Black, 2003), chap. 2. For a variety of perspectives, also see S.P. Gupta and K.S. Ramachandran (eds.) *Mahabharata: Myth and Reality: Differing views* (Delhi, Agam Prakashan, 1976).

'text-aided archaeology' was that these archaeologists were unable to recognize the significance of sites that were not mentioned in ancient literature. This is the reason why, in spite of all his knowledge and experience, Alexander Cunningham was unable to understand the tremendous significance of Harappa.

'Epic archaeology' became more prominent in post-independence India. The most important excavations of an 'epic site' were those at Hastinapura in 1950–2. The report of the excavations, published by B.B. Lal in 1954–5, remains an important landmark. It documented the long sequence of archaeological cultures in the upper Ganga–Yamuna doab, with a meticulous presentation of details of artefacts (especially pottery), and a careful analysis of bone and plant remains.[20] Lal also tried to correlate evidence from the site with events linked to the *Mahabharata* legend. For instance, he suggested that the flood-line that marked the end of the Painted Grey Ware (PGW) settlement at Hastinapura could represent the flood during Nichakshu's reign, mentioned in the *Vishnu Purana*, as a result of which, the Pandavas' descendents had to shift their capital to Kaushambi. While the mass of archaeological data marshalled in the Hastinapura report remains an important addition to archaeological knowledge, the specific connections that Lal tried to establish between the site and epic-puranic legends remain highly speculative.

Connecting epic legends with history is part of a larger issue of how to correlate evidence from ancient literature with archaeology. While many historians decry attempts to correlate archaeological sites with epic events, they themselves correlate pottery types with groups of people such as the Indo-Aryans or with Puranic lineages.[21] Linking the

---

[20] B.B. Lal, 'Excavation at Hastinapura and other Explorations in the Upper Ganga and Sutlej Basins 1950–52, *Ancient India: Bulletin of the Archaeological Survey of India*, nos 10 and 11 (1954 and 1955), pp. 5–151.

[21] See, for instance, R.S. Sharma, *Material Culture and Social Formations in Ancient India* (Delhi, Macmillan India, 1983), chap. 4 and Romila Thapar, 'Puranic Lineages and Archaeological Cultures, *Puratattva*, 8 (1975), pp. 86–98.

creations of literary and historical imagination with material remains of the past is no easy or straight-forward task. Historians and archaeologists have to reflect carefully about just what sorts of connections can and cannot be made between archaeological cultures and groups of people.

The Intersections between the Ancient, Medieval and Modern:
The Medieval History of the Ashokan Pillars

When we divide the past into segments such as ancient, medieval, and modern, we often miss out on the connections between them. We ignore the multiple and diverse layers of meaning that historical artefacts and monuments attract over time. Of course ancient artefacts had '*original*' locations, meanings, and functions, but their complex life histories often led them very far away from these. The historical landscape of Delhi offers many instances of what I refer to in the last chapter of this book as 'the mingling of the ages'. I find this mingling one of the most exciting aspects of the history of any place, one that reminds us that the remains of the past are constantly infused with new meanings in the present. This is an important issue that needs elaboration and reflection.

In ancient India, free-standing pillars sometimes marked shrines or religious places. Or they could be bearers of royal messages or victory emblems, engraved with accounts of the greatness and achievements of kings. Such pillars were sometimes reused during the reigns of later kings in ancient as well as medieval times. The three ancient pillars that stand in Delhi today are striking instances of this practice.

The Delhi-Topra pillar stands majestically on top of a three-storeyed building in Feroz Shah Kotla. Its long smooth shaft has a number of inscriptions, including seven edicts on *dhamma* (piety), inscribed in the third century BC during the reign of the Maurya emperor Ashoka, as well as five medieval inscriptions. The Delhi–Meerut pillar opposite

Bara Hindu Rao Hospital has six Ashokan edicts on *dhamma* as well as three short early medieval inscriptions.[22] Medieval chronicles record the fact that these pillars were brought to Delhi from Topra and Meerut during the time of Sultan Firuz Shah Tughluq in the fourteenth century.[23] An anonymous Persian text called the *Sirat-i-Firuz Shahi*, also written during Firuz Shah's reign, gives more details about how the Topra pillar was moved to Delhi. A manuscript of the *Sirat* that found its way into the Oriental Public Library in Patna actually has illustrations showing the various stages of the operations.[24]

Firuz Shah chose the location of both pillars with care. He had the Delhi–Topra pillar installed in the citadel of his city of Firozabad, the significance of which is self-evident. The Delhi–Meerut pillar was installed in the Sultan's hunting palace. There is a two-storeyed structure made of rubble masonry on the northern ridge, very close to where the Delhi–Meerut pillar now stands. This structure, known variously as the Kushk-i-Shikar, Pirghaib, Jahanuma, or the Observatory is believed to represent the site of Firuz Shah Tughluq's hunting palace.

The pillars were considered as marvels, not as war trophies. This is clear from the circumstances in which they were found, moved and the way in which they are described.[25] The fact that the *Tarikh-i-Firuz Shahi* and the *Sirat-i-Firuz Shahi* give so many details of the moving and installation of the Delhi-Topra pillar suggests that it had an important symbolic significance for Firoz Shah. The pillar was installed in front of the Jama Masjid in Firoz Shah Kotla and a bridge may have

[22] On the post-Maurya history of Ashoka's pillars see Upinder Singh, 'Texts on Stone: understanding Asoka's epigraph-monuments and their changing contexts' *Indian Historical Review*, 24 (1998), pp. 1–19.

[23] The account of the moving of the pillars in Shams Siraj Afif's *Tarikh-i-Firuz-Shahi* is discussed in Chapter 5 of this book.

[24] J.A. Page, *A Memoir on Kotla Firoz Shah, Delhi*, with a translation of Sirat-i-Firozshahi by Muhammad Hamid Kuraishi (Memoirs of the Archaeological Survey of India, No. 52) (originally published in 1937, 1999 reprint edn, New Delhi, Archaeological Survey of India), Plate VI.

[25] Kuraishi in Page, *op. cit.*, p. 33.

connected the two. In its new home, the pillar came to be known as a *minar* (tower), reflecting its new symbolic connection with the mosque. As for the location of the pillar installed in, on or near Firuz Shah's hunting palace, it is important to remember that hunting was not simply a leisure past-time for medieval elites. It had an important place in notions of sovereignty in medieval India.[26]

Firuz Shah may have gone to great lengths to relocate Ashokan pillars because he was impressed by the technical skill involved in crafting them, their beauty and majesty. But there was surely something more. In spite of the older inscriptions not being readable, the more recent ones could be read at the time, for the *Sirat* mentions that one of them belonged to the reign of the Chauhan king Visaladeva. Firuz Shah's dealings with the Ashokan pillars suggest some general sort of comprehension of the importance of such pillars, even if the text of their oldest inscriptions and the *precise* nature of their original significance and function would no longer have been known.[27]

The Medieval History of the Mehrauli Iron Pillar

Most people who live in Delhi know about the iron pillar which stands in the Jami Masjid in the Qutb complex in Mehrauli. The pillar once stood in the precincts of a Vishnu temple, and its earliest inscription is in all likelihood a *prashasti* (eulogy) of the Gupta king

---

[26] For an elaboration on the significance of the royal hunt for the Mughals, see Ebba Koch, *Mughal Art and Imperial Ideology: Collected Essays* (New Delhi, Oxford University Press, 2001), pp. 177–9.

[27] Parts of Ashoka's pillars are also found in two other cities built by Firoz Shah—Hissar Firoza and Fatehabad (both in Haryana). In the former place, the fragment of an Ashokan pillar forms the lowest part of a composite pillar standing in front of a mosque known as the Lat ki Masjid, built during the time of Firuz Shah. At Fatehabad, the Ashokan fragment is part of a composite pillar located in the middle of a praying ground with a late Mughal wall. This pillar has a Persian inscription giving Firuz Shah's genealogy (Harry Falk, 'A Neglected Pillar of Asoka', *South Asian Archaeology*, vol. 1, 1995, pp. 429–38). The credit for first suggesting that the Hissar and Fatehabad fragments seem to be two parts of one and the same pillar goes to Alexander Cunningham (*Archaeological Survey Reports,* vol. 5, *Report for the Year 1872–3,* Calcutta, 1875. p. 142).

Chandragupta II (375–413 AD). Chemical analysis has shown the pillar to be made of pure wrought iron (99.7% iron) with a very low sulphur and very high phosphorus content. Considerable metallurgical skill must have been required to forge such a long piece of iron, and the inscriptions are still extremely clear. What is considered most remarkable is the fact that the pillar has remained comparatively rust-free even after so many centuries. There is evidence of rusting on the areas where it was exposed to prolonged contact with water—the underground and the topmost part, where water can accumulate in the grooves.[28] Like the Ashokan pillars, the iron pillar bears several short inscriptions apart from the 'main' one. These include an eleventh century inscription which refers to the Tomara king Anangapala establishing Delhi.[29]

It is not certain whether the iron pillar is *in situ* or not. It may have been situated here or nearby right from the start, but there are theories that identify its original location near the source of the Beas, or at Udayagiri in central India or Gaya in Bihar. If the pillar was moved here from somewhere else, who was responsible for moving it? The *Tarikh-i-Firuz Shahi* states it was set up in this position by Iltutmish. This event may have taken place in around 1229, when the mosque was enlarged.[30] Afif also indicates that it was Iltutmish's example that inspired Firuz Shah to relocate and reuse old pillars.[31]

Ancient pillars attracted the attention of the Mughal emperors as well. The remarkable Ashokan pillar in the Allahabad fort has inscriptions of Ashoka, the Gupta emperor Samudragupta, and the Mughal emperor Jahangir. In his memoirs, Jahangir mentions a pillar at Dhar in Madhya Pradesh. This can be identified with fragments of

[28] For these and other details, see M.C. Joshi (ed.) *King Chandra and the Meharauli Pillar* (Meerut, Kusumanjali Prakashan, 1989).
[29] The manner in which the Gupta iron pillar got entangled in folklore connected with the naming of Delhi is discussed in Chapter 7 of this book.
[30] Finbarr B. Flood, Pillars, Palimpsests, and Princely Practices,' *Islamic Arts, Anthropology and Aesthetics*, Res 43, Spring 2003, pp. 99–100.
[31] Flood, *op. cit.*, p. 100.

a large iron pillar (over 13 m) with a Sanskrit inscription which lies in front of a mosque at Dhar. The pillar may have originally been a *jayastambha* (victory pillar) erected by a Paramara ruler in the twelfth or thirteenth century. It seems to have been relocated and erected in front of the mosque in 1404. It may have fallen when a sixteenth century ruler named Sultan Bahadur tried to remove it and carry it off to Gujarat. An inscription—inscribed after it had fallen—records Jahangir halting here. The Mughal emperor apparently wanted to take largest piece to Agra to use as a lamp stand, but never got round to doing so.[32]

Clearly, there is much more to Firuz Shah's penchant for ancient pillars than meets the eye! Finbarr B. Flood makes an interesting and persuasive argument that such pillars had a trans-cultural significance. He suggests that while the construction of the Qutb mosque clearly involved the reuse and reassembling of temple pillars which can be understood as war spolia, the iron pillar is different and cannot be considered as a war trophy. Like the Ashokan pillars moved to Delhi on the orders of Firuz Shah, it was part of an attempt of the early Delhi sultans to connect themselves with the royal traditions of India's ancient past.[33]

The Modern History of the Ashokan Pillars

If the medieval history of the Ashokan pillars that stand today in Delhi was eventful, the modern history of the Delhi–Meerut pillar is even more so. Its rough and ravaged look bears testimony to this. Writing in the 1860s, Alexander Cunningham describes the pillar as lying in five pieces near Hindu Rao's house on the top of a hill on the Delhi ridge. This house was built by William Fraser, Agent to the Governor

---

[32] Catherine B. Asher, 'Appropriating the Past: Jahangir's Pillars,' *Islamic Culture*, 71, no. 4 (1997), p. 8.

[33] Flood., *op. cit.*, p. 95, Interesting and insightful as this observation is, there is the question of just how important such strategies were in the notions of sovereignty projected by the Delhi sultans or the Mughals.

General at Delhi. When Fraser was murdered by Shams-ud-din Khan, nawab of Ferozpur, it was bought by a Maratha nobleman named Hindu Rao. The site of the house is now marked by Bara Hindu Rao Hospital and some of the old parts of the building can still be identified. A British garrison was stationed here in 1857, and this spot was a major scene of action during the revolt that broke out in that year.

It is believed that the pillar had broken into pieces due to the accidental explosion of a magazine of gun-powder in the early eighteenth century during the reign of the Mughal emperor Farukhsiyar. On the other hand, Beglar tells us that 'native tradition' asserts that it was thrown down by William Fraser, to build his house on the site, and that some old men said that they had actually seen it standing. In Beglar's opinion, this was yet another example 'of how difficult, if not impossible it is to place the slightest reliance on native accounts, especially those which ascribe some act of vandalism to their European conquerors'.[34]

Anyway, no doubt since he had bought the piece of property on or near which the pillar once stood, its fragments came into the possession of Hindu Rao, who presented them to the museum of the Asiatic Society of Bengal. One part of the middle, which was inscribed with Ashoka's edicts, was sawn off by the executive engineer of Delhi and despatched to Calcutta. In 1866, it was sent back to Delhi and the pieces were joined together. The gist of this long story is given on a plaque set up by the Archaeological Survey of India at the base of the pillar.

Today, the Kushk-i-shikar is known in the area not because of its association with Firuz Shah, but with a *pir*. A cenotaph, covered with a *chadar* and offerings of incense sticks and flowers, gives ample evidence of the continuing worship of the pir. Local tradition includes stories of the pir having been sighted at this place, riding a camel.

---

[34] Beglar and Carlleyle, *op. cit.*, pp. 2–3.

There is also a *baba* (an old, wise man) who comes here regularly every
Thursday, offering advice on various personal problems to a following
consisting of Hindus and Muslims from various areas, including
Chandrawal, near Majnu ka tila. The Baba claims to be the third in
his line and claims that his grandfather established his base at this spot
after 1857.[35]

When I visited the three-storeyed structure which supports the
Ashokan pillar at Feroz Shah Kotla in February 2006, incense sticks
and petitions written out on paper, addressed to Kotwali Baba or Dada
Miyan, marked the blackened walls of its many niches. The petitions
describe personal travails, illness, a wayward child, a failed business.
As for the Ashokan pillar itself, vandals seem to have switched from
inscribing to using a more ephemeral medium—chalk. Apart from the
mandatory hearts and declarations of undying love, I noted the name
of Shahrukh Khan chalked in by a star-struck fan. Also chalked onto
the pillar was the poignant, heart-felt plea: '*Ya Allah! Paper mein achchhe
number aayen!*' (Oh God! May I get high marks in my examination!)

Anand Taneja's on-going research on the history of Firoz Shah
Kotla, which includes a documention of the oral traditions connected
with this place, gives further fascinating details.[36] Believers consider
the stone structure at Firoz Shah Kotla to be inhabited by many *jinns*—
mischievous, supernatural beings who are capable of manifesting
themselves to the pious and helping those in distress. The most
important of these jinns is known as Lat-wale-Baba (Baba of the pillar).
Taneja suggests that the petitioning of jinns at this place seems to have
either started or resumed in the 1970s and is associated with a man
named Laddu Shah. The activity has picked up during the last seven
or eight years. Many of the devout come from the old city, but some
from as far away as Ghaziabad. It is interesting to note that this

---

[35] This information is from Anand Taneja, personal communication.
[36] This research is not yet published. The following information is based on personal communication.

interaction with the jinns takes place right next door to the orthodox worship at the nearby mosque, which has a small congregation. There is also a *dargah* (grave) of a Chishti saint in the vicinity, with its own circle of devotees. The caretaker of the dargah, Muhammad Ahmad Chishti, gave Taneja his own unusual take on the inscriptions on the Ashokan pillar. According to him, they recorded an alchemical formula to turn base metal into gold, to be revealed on the day when no evil remains in the hearts of men.

In the modern history of the Ashokan pillars, we have a fascinating combination of diverse elements—an ancient pillar, a medieval monument, modern traditions of local pir and jinn worship, structures that attract diverse expressions of deep and desperate human angst. Why do certain artefacts, monuments, structures (both religious and non-religious) have a propensity to attract such sacralization over the centuries? Does it have to do with their age, their appearance, their aura, the level of their unknownness and mystery? Do they somehow manage to convey an inchoate sense of history and authority that transcends time, one that is felt but not clearly understood, and which is capable of undergoing many transformations?

Why is it that the Kushk-i-Shikar has attracted such sacralization, and the Mutiny Memorial just down the road hasn't? Is the Mutiny Memorial too recent, too clearly understood, too small and compact, too well-preserved? Is it too complete to leave spaces for popular imagination to fill in with reflections of human yearnings and anxieties? Is it because it lacks dark nooks and crannies where people can pray and leave offerings in solitude? Or is it because it has so far not been touched by a holy man or a miracle whose memory still fires popular imagination?[37]

---

[37] The Mutiny Memorial was not sacralized, but it did get eventually nationalized in 1972. A plaque at the base of the monument announces in Hindi, Urdu, English, and Gurmukhi that the 'enemies' implied by the inscriptions on the memorial in colonial times were not rebels but brave freedom fighters.

Historical remains are important windows into the history of their times. But they have other meanings as well. Some become spaces that are shared harmoniously by different communities. Others get politicized and become contested spaces, sources of bitter strife and conflict. In their more benign roles, they are tourist destinations, favoured picnic spots, meeting-spots for lovers, and venues for hosting state events. Monuments such as the Qutb and the Purana Qila today provide chic and evocative backgrounds for music and dance performances. All this demonstrates that historical monuments are cultural resources with an impressive capacity to taken on many different, often unusual, roles and meanings.

Introduction to the First Edition

Histories of Delhi narrate a history of cities, seven or more in number. Starting with Indraprastha of the *Mahabharata* legend, they usually take a gigantic leap of almost two thousand years into the eighth century AD when the Tomara Rajputs moved into the hills south of Delhi to found the settlement of Anangpur and later, the citadel of Lal Kot. Little is said of what was happening in the Delhi area during the thousands of years *before* the terrible *Mahabharata* war (if the war ever happened, that is) and what transpired during the centuries between this war and the coming of the Rajputs.

There *is*, in fact, enough available evidence for us to weave a connected account of Delhi's ancient past. This evidence reveals that the history of Delhi is not simply a story of cities built at different sites at different times but a history of many settlements, some urban, many more rural in nature. In its earliest part, it goes back to a distant time before cities or settled villages had emerged.

As ancient and modern boundaries do not coincide, it is a good idea to be liberal in demarcating the region that we intend to look at. This will include not only modern Old and New Delhi but also neighbouring areas such as the Faridabad district of Haryana and

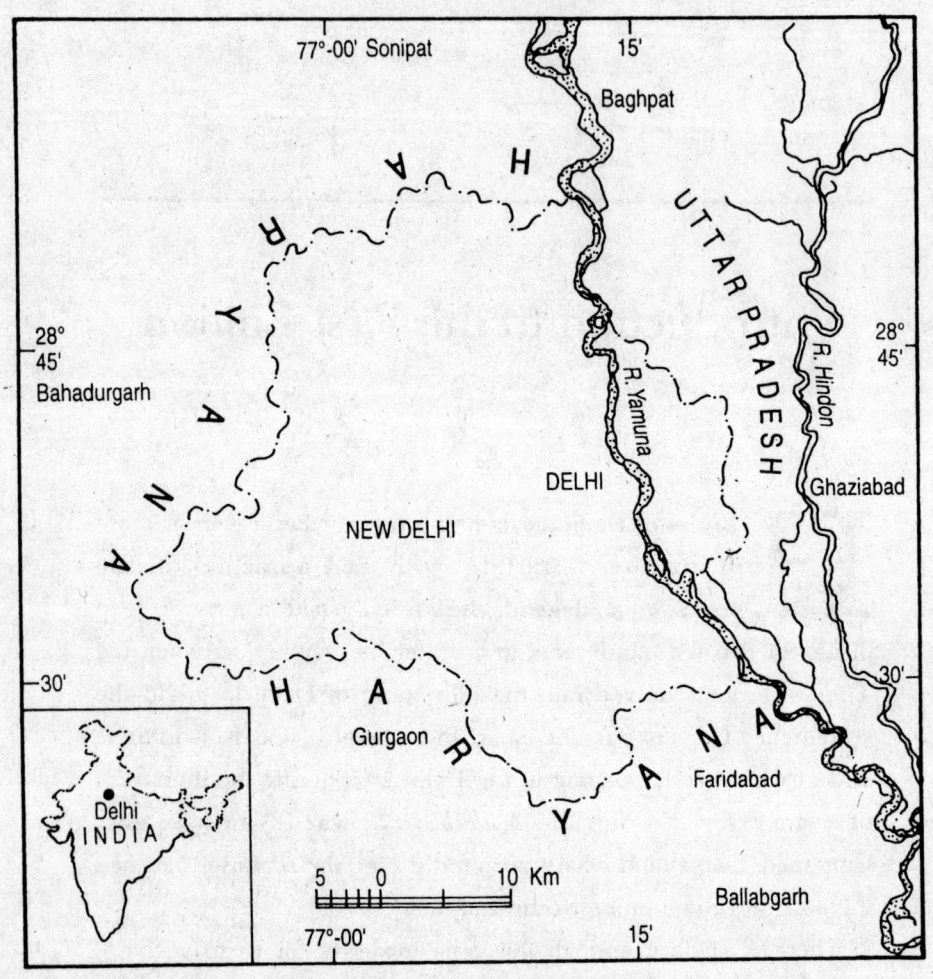

Delhi and neighbouring areas

the Ghaziabad district of Uttar Pradesh. The selection of this broader area can be justified on geographical and historical grounds and has the advantage of giving us a wide canvas to work on.

Before beginning the story of Delhi's ancient past, we need to pause and consider how we get to know this past. Ancient literature, much of it religious in nature, gives us occasional glimpses into Delhi's early history. Unfortunately, the dates of many of the texts are uncertain and the information they give is often a complex synthesis of mythology and historical fact. Literature also tends to speak for those periods when the capital of a kingdom lay in the Delhi area, but is otherwise silent.

This is where archaeology steps in. The archaeological evidence for the history of medieval Delhi is very visible in the form of impressive monuments of various kinds—forts, mosques, tombs, and the like. The story of Delhi's *ancient* past, on the other hand, lies mostly underground, concealed by layers of accumulated soil and debris. It reveals itself when disturbed either by accident or by the deliberate intrusion of the archaeologist's spade.

A striking aspect of many ancient Indian cities and villages is their impressive antiquity. In the plains, old sites are often marked by mounds, wherever these have not been destroyed by activities such as farming or the construction of houses, factories, and roads. There are several old mounds in and around Delhi. Some of these indicate occupation over centuries. In places where the mound gets disturbed or cut away, such as when someone decides to build a house or to level the ground to grow crops on, the remains of ancient times are exposed.

Archaeology can tell us a great deal about the everyday lives of people—what they ate, how they obtained their food, the houses they built and lived in, the pots they made and used, the crafts they specialized in, and their contacts with other people. It can also give us clues about certain aspects of their social, political, and religious life. Unfortunately very few ancient Indian sites have been excavated horizontally (i.e. over a large surface area) and detailed reports of excavations are not always published. Hence, the archaeological evidence that is available often gives us tantalizing clues rather than a large volume of detailed information. Apart from sites, other sources of information on the past of the Delhi area are the stray, isolated finds of different sorts of artefacts (an artefact is any object that has been made or altered by human hands) from various places.

The history of an area is not only what the literary and archaeological sources reveal to the historian. We should not ignore what people remember of their past, how they interpret it and connect themselves with it. Hence, the history of Delhi includes the story of orally transmitted local legends and traditions which are recorded not in written texts but in collective memory. In remembering and recreating the past in various ways, people transform it into something that is meaningful in their lives and in the present.

1

The Altered Landscape

If we want to understand the life of ancient people, we must
know something about the world in which they lived. The
physical environment, which includes topography, climate,
flora, fauna, and mineral resources, does not *determine* human
activity, but it does lay down certain conditions within which human
beings operate and with which they have to grapple in order to
live. Environmental conditions played a particularly important role
during the earliest phases of the human past when people had a
comparatively limited (compared to modern times, that is)
repertoire of resources and skills with which to manipulate their
surroundings. It is important to remember that environments have
not been the same through time, and that ancient landscapes and
climates were very often dramatically different from modern ones.
Such changes in environments have been the result of natural
factors in some cases and human activity and interference in others.

Delhi gets its strategic importance from its peculiar geographical
position. It lies in the corridor between the Himalayas in the north
and the Aravalli hills and Thar desert of Rajasthan to the south
and south-west. Delhi is also located in one of the important
watershed zones of north India—that which divides the two great

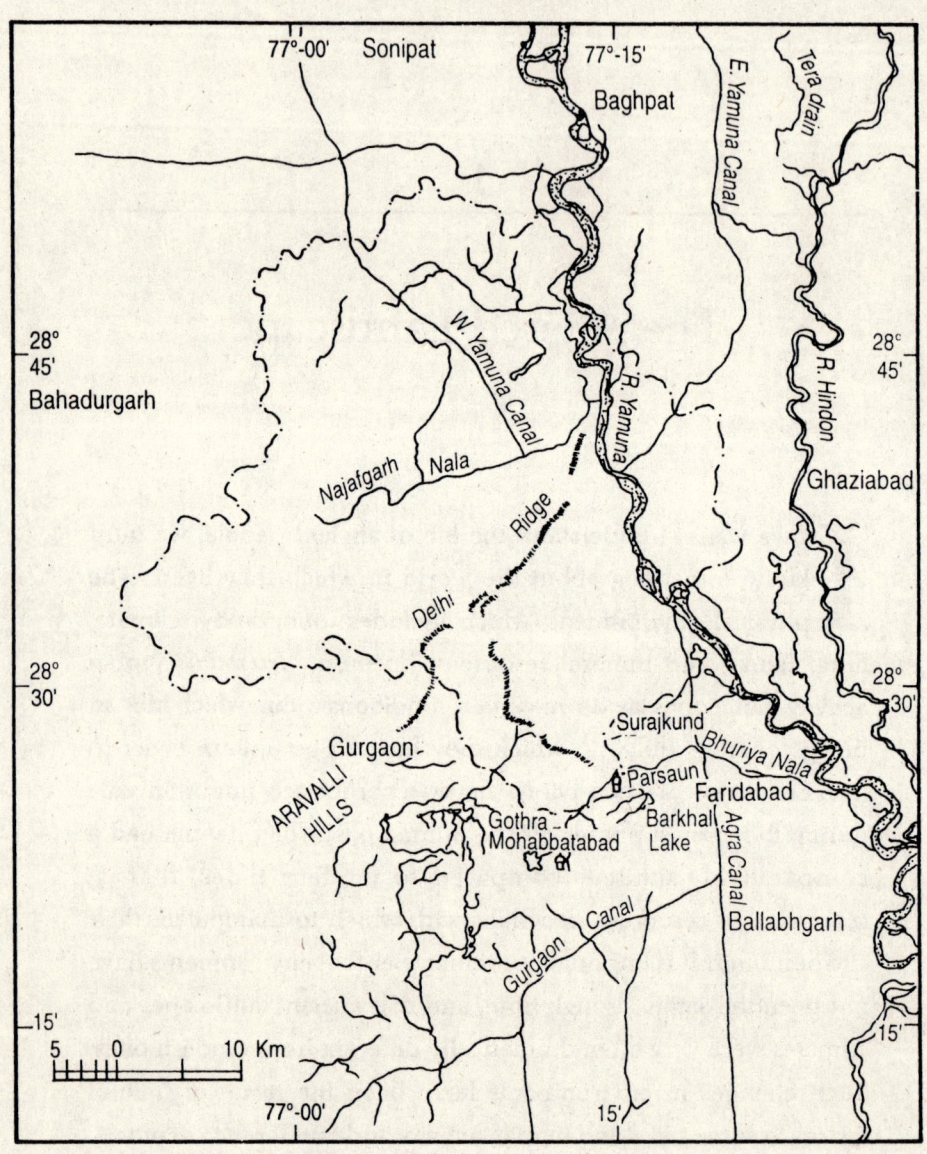

Delhi: the physical environment

river systems of the Indus and the Ganga. It is the gateway to the vast alluvial plain created by the Ganga and its tributaries.

The 1883–4 Gazetteer of the Delhi District introduces its description of the Delhi tract with restraint, remarking that the area '...though exhibiting none of the beauties of mountainous districts, possesses a considerable diversity of physical feature, and in parts is not wanting in picturesqueness.'[1] This picturesqueness, it goes on to add, is due to the hills and the Yamuna river. The landscape of Delhi consists of the alluvial plain of the Yamuna interrupted in places by low-lying, rocky hills and plateaux.

The hills of the Delhi Ridge

The hills that form the Delhi Ridge (locally known as *kohi* or *pahari*) are the northernmost extensions of the Aravallis, the oldest mountain range in India. An arm of the Aravallis enters Delhi from Gurgaon in the south, and runs through the city in a north-easterly direction, ending at Wazirabad on the right bank of the Yamuna. The Ridge has four sections: the southern Ridge (outside city limits), the south-central Ridge in the Mehrauli area, the central/ New Delhi Ridge north of Dhaula Kuan, and the northern/Old Delhi Ridge between Civil Lines and the University of Delhi.

The Aravallis, which attain an impressive height of 1722 m. at Mount Abu in Rajasthan are reduced to very modest proportions as they peter out in Delhi. Here, their height ranges from 2.5 m. above the Yamuna plains in the north to a maximum of about 90 m. above plain level in the south. However, what we see are the highly eroded remains of a once imposing mountain range. Today, the southern stretches of the Ridge provide a variety of building and road-making materials such as quartzite and *kankar* (a

[1] Gazetteer of the Delhi District, 1883–4; 2nd ed. (New Delhi, 1988), p. 1.

calcareous concrete). Unfortunately, it is this very economic potential that is responsible for the rapid destruction of both the rocky hillsides and historical sites situated on them.

The thorn scrub forest of the Northern and Central Ridge is to a large extent a modern creation. It is the result of the interplay of two factors—the afforestation launched by the British colonial government in the late-nineteenth and early-twentieth centuries and the subsequent steady depletion of the vegetation due to exploitation.[2] The original vegetation can be reconstructed by looking to the Aravallis of Rajasthan which support a variety of dry, tropical forest species some of which are now very rare on the Delhi Ridge.[3] Today, the Ridge supports trees such as the *babul* (*Acacia nilotica*), *phulahi* (*Acacia modesta*), *katha* (*Acacia catechu*), and *Acacia senegal* and shrubs such as *bansa* (*Adhatoda vasica*), *heens* (*Capparis sepiaria*), and *jangli karaunda* (*Carissa spinarum*). Naturalized exotic species include the *kabuli* or *vilayati kikar* (*Prosopis juliflora*), native to Mexico and Central America, which was introduced on the Delhi Ridge in the early-twentieth-century. Encroachments, in the form of unauthorized construction, grazing, and tree-felling pose serious threats to the Delhi Ridge forest today.

The Yamuna and lesser streams

Beyond the hills and forest, towards the east, there is the river.

---

[2] The initial steps towards large-scale tree-planting on the Northern and Central Ridge were taken a few years after the 1857 Mutiny. The major afforestation was initiated after 1912 by the Town Planning Committee of the newly formed Delhi Administration, under the direction of William Robertson Mustoe. On Lutyens' urging, the central and northern sections of the Ridge were fenced in and declared Reserve Forests. (*The Delhi Ridge Forest: Decline and Conservation*, Kalpavriksha, New Delhi, 1991, p.2).

[3] For details of the flora of the Ridge (and Delhi in general), *see* J.K. Maheshwari, *The Flora of Delhi* (Council of Scientific and Industrial Research, New Delhi, 1963). Also, *The Delhi Ridge Forest*.

The Yamuna is a perennial river flowing north-south through Delhi. In the dry summers its depth may be no more than four feet at places but during the monsoon rains the river swells into a fierce torrent, prone to floods. The alluvial plain of the Yamuna today supports a variety of agricultural and horticultural activity. Local rural terminology divides the Yamuna alluvium into two parts— the *khadar* (the new alluvium, bordering the present course of the river) and the *bangar* (the old alluvium, representing the alluvial soil accumulated by the river in its earlier courses). The *dabar* is the low-lying, rain-fed area lying to the west of the hills.

The Yamuna is a temperamental river, and has changed its course dramatically during its history due to factors such as tectonic movements. It is supposed to have once flowed into the Saraswati (identified with the modern Ghaggar–Hakra), eulogized as the foremost of all rivers in the ancient hymns of the *Rig Veda*. Over time, it preferred to chart a more and more easterly course, eventually abandoning the Saraswati and joining up with the system of the Ganga. The remains of at least six palaeo-channels (old channels or courses) of the Yamuna have been identified in the Delhi area. Traces of old courses of the river can be seen in various lakes such as the Najafgarh, Surajkund and Barkhal lakes. Studies of the palaeo-channels have shown that the migration of the river ranged over about 100 km. in the north and west Delhi region to 40 km. in the south. The evidence suggests that the Yamuna once flowed through the hills south of Delhi. It seems to have abandoned its hilly route around 4000 years ago, gradually moving eastwards through the plains area till it settled into its present course.[4] The migration of the Yamuna is a very important part of the history of ancient settlements in the Delhi region. While many stone age

---

[4] *See* A.K. Grover and P.L. Bakliwal, 'A Study of Yamuna River through Remote Sensing,' *Man and Environment,* 9 (1985)· pp 151–3.

sites have been found in the hilly stretches that were once traversed
by it, several ancient mounds mark settlements that grew up along
the older courses of the river.

Apart from the Yamuna river, several smaller streams form
part of the drainage of the Delhi area. These streams emerge from
the Aravalli stretches in the Ballabgarh region south of Delhi, and
generally flow in an easterly direction. One of the most important
is the Bhuriya nala, which flows eastwards from the hills near
Anangpur, through the plains, to join up with the Yamuna. While
some of the old streams have become extinct, others are today
subdued versions of what they once were, due to the building of
bunds (embankments) and canals. Nevertheless, several ancient
sites located in their catchment areas and along their courses point
to their importance as water sources in earlier times.

The Yamuna (also known as the Kalindi) has a special place in
Indian religious geography. The river is personified as a goddess
in ancient texts. A hymn in the *Rig Veda Samhita* (10. 10) speaks
of Yami who loved her twin brother Yama (god of the dead in
later Indian mythology) a little too passionately. The *Puranas*
elaborate on the genealogy of the twins, describing them as children
of the Sun by Samjna, and identify Yami with the river Yamuna.
In the *Mahabharata*, the Yamuna is a sacred river. In the course of
their tour of important places of pilgrimage (*tirthas*), Yudhishthira
is urged by the sage Lomasha to bathe in the Yamuna, the gateway
to Kurukshetra. In doing so, Lomasha tells him, he will see all the
worlds before his eyes and will be cleansed of all sins. Many spots
along the Yamuna are described in the epic as the places where
kings and sages of ancient times performed sacrifices.

In the *Vishnu Purana*, an intoxicated Balarama (the elder brother
of Krishna) commands the river Yamuna to draw near to him to
enable him to bathe. Yamuna ignores his order, upon which

Balarama throws his ploughshare into the river and drags her waters towards him, till the recalcitrant river is forced to beg his forgiveness. In some other *Puranas*, the god Shiva, roaming grief-stricken and agitated after the death of his consort Sati, plunges into the Kalindi, turning its clear water black.

The goddess Yamuna is depicted along with Ganga in the sculpture of many ancient Indian temples, often flanking their entrance. Ganga, white as the moon, stands on a *matsya* (fish) or *makara* (crocodile). Yamuna is the dark goddess. She stands on a *kachchhapa* (tortoise). The two goddesses sometimes hold a *chamara* (fly-whisk) in one hand and a flower in the other. Elsewhere, they may be seen wielding a *purna-kumbha* (jar of plenty).

It is curious that although the Yamuna is recognized as a great river in ancient religious texts, no major sacred shrine or cult spot (leaving aside the Nili Chhatri temple) is located on the banks of this river in the Delhi area. On the other hand, several places that are important in current local religious geography can be found along the small streams that meander through the Ballabgarh hills south of Delhi. Some of these sacred places lay claim to great antiquity by linking themselves with famous *rishis* or sages known from ancient Sanskrit texts. In a ravine located at the source of the Parsaun stream is a place where, according to local tradition, the ancient *rishi* Parashara performed his *tapasya* (religious austerities). At the source of another hill stream (locally known as the Ganga), in the hills a few kilometres west of Pali, is Gothra–Mohabbatabad. The priests of the temple complex here declare it to be the place where Uddalaka *rishi* of Upanishadic fame sat in *tapasya*; visitors are shown the small cave where the seer sat in meditation. A beautiful *mukhalinga* (the phallic emblem of the god Shiva with his face sculpted on it) which stylistically seems to belong to the early Gupta phase (about the fourth century AD) suggests that this may well be an ancient religious place.[5]

Ancient flora and fauna

We do not have detailed studies of the ancient plant and animal life of Delhi. But a glance at the much later nineteenth century literature on the subject is startling: it tells us how radically the flora and fauna of Delhi has changed within the last century and a half. The 1883–4 *Gazetteer of the Delhi District* speaks of a tree cover that was much more extensive than it is today. It talks of pigs, foxes, and hares along the banks of the Yamuna, *chinkara* in the north-eastern parts of the district especially on the Ridge, gentle *nilgai* grazing in various areas, wolves roaming around the cantonment area, monkeys making a nuisance of themselves in villages bordering the Western Yamuna canal, and leopards prowling about in the outlying villages. Black buck, jackal, peafowl, duck, quail, snipe, *kulan,* partridge, hedge-hog, mongoose, and snakes were in abundance everywhere. The *Gazetteer* tells us that cobra-hunting in the Old Fort was a common past-time for soldiers of the British garrison, especially in the rainy season or just before its onset. It lists the various types of fish found in the Yamuna river, and talks of the entire river being infested with crocodiles. 'In that part of the river opposite the present rifle range,' the *Gazetteer* informs us, 'they may be seen any afternoon in hundreds swimming about or basking on the edge of the water. Between the old fort and Okhlah, they are equally numerous.'[5]

The account of Delhi's fauna in the more recent 1976 *Delhi Gazetteer* is much less exciting. It lists the hyena, wolf, fox, jackal, leopard, black buck, gazelle, *nilgai,* and otters among the fauna of

[5] See pp. 55–6 and photograph
[6] *Gazetteer of the Delhi District,* 1883–4, p. 21.

the region, but their numbers had obviously dwindled drastically (as they have continued to do over the last few decades). Due to the steady expansion of human settlement and activity in the area, Delhi's fauna today presents a rather pathetic picture compared to the late-nineteenth-century image of an area thronging with so many species of animals, fish, and fowl. We can only imagine how dramatically abundant and different the flora and fauna of the Delhi area must have been thousands of years ago.

2

The Testimony of Stone Tools

T he story of the human past begins in an age when stone was the most important raw material used by people. The stone age goes back to over a million years ago, to a time before modern humans–*Homo sapiens sapiens*–had evolved. On the basis of geological age, types of stone tools and tool-making techniques, and means of obtaining food, archaeologists divide stone age cultures into three phases—the palaeolithic, mesolithic, and neolithic. These three phases do not have a uniform time-frame in the world or in the Indian subcontinent. The palaeolithic age corresponds to the pleistocene era of the history of the earth, which may have begun between 3 million and 1.7 million years ago. It was an age when humans and their *hominid* (i.e. man-like) ancestors obtained their food through hunting and gathering. On the basis of changes in stone tools and techniques, the palaeolithic is further sub-divided into the lower, middle, and upper palaeolithic cultures.

The pleistocene era came to an end about ten thousand years ago and made way for the holocene era, which continues into our own time. Archaeologists use the term mesolithic for stone age cultures of the holocene era that lived mainly by hunting and food-gathering and had developed the skills to make various types of small stone tools or microliths. The term 'neolithic' refers to stone-age cultures that had developed certain specialized techniques of polishing, pecking, and grinding stone tools and which had taken the very important step towards food production based on domesticating plants and animals. We are looking at an enormous span of time during which humans (and before them *hominids*) in different parts of the world evolved biologically and culturally, developing various levels of skills and techniques in their interaction with the environment and with each other.

What do we know about the prehistoric past of the Delhi region? Numerous finds of stone tools in the stretches of the Aravallis in and around Delhi give evidence of the presence and activities of stone age people right from the lower palaeolithic phase. Dates are difficult to give, but we seem to be looking at a period beginning roughly about 100,000 years ago. Unfortunately, no skeletal remains of these prehistoric people have been found in the Delhi area so far. The evidence consists entirely of stone tools.

As already suggested, it is important to remember that the environment of Delhi that meets our eye today is very different from that experienced by stone age humans who lived here thousands of years ago. In their time, the hillsides of the Delhi Ridge would have been higher and more densely wooded, home to a plant and animal life very different from that of today. The ruins of Sultan Firuz Shah Tughluq's hunting palace, somewhat incongruously located within the compound of the Hindu Rao Hospital, suggest that as late as in the fourteenth century the game available on the Ridge near the University of Delhi was enough to qualify for a king's hunt. How much more abundant the wild life must have been here thousands of years ago when prehistoric men, women, and children roamed the terrain! The hilly stretches

of the Aravallis, especially where they were watered by hill streams,
offered stone age inhabitants certain important attractions. Apart
from the food that the vegetation and animal life provided, these
stretches also provided rock out of which prehistoric people
fashioned their stone tools. The fact that so many prehistoric stone
tools have been found in various places in these hills, and will no
doubt continue to be found, shows that this terrain was attractive
to prehistoric people from various points of view.

Stone age sites in the Delhi area
The first stone age tool in Delhi was discovered in 1956, when
Surajit Sinha found four lower palaeolithic tools on the Ridge near
the main gate of the University of Delhi. In 1974, the great Indian
archaeologist H.D. Sankalia reported the discovery of some more
palaeolithic tools on the Delhi Ridge. In 1983, B.M. Pande found
a late Acheulian hand-axe (the Acheulian is an advanced technique
of making hand-axes) on the campus of Jawaharlal Nehru
University. These stone tools gave definite evidence of the presence
and activities of stone age humans in the Delhi area. In 1985–6,
D.K. Chakrabarti and N. Lahiri made a systematic survey of stone
age sites in south Delhi and adjacent parts of Haryana and located
as many as 43 sites, ranging from the lower palaeolithic to
microlithic. One of the sites in the hills of the Jawaharlal Nehru
University campus was identified as possibly being a lower
palaeolithic factory site, i.e., a site where stone tools were actually
made.[7] While the earlier finds had suggested the rather curious
connection of prehistoric remains with two modern centres of
higher learning, this study proved that this was just a coincidence.
Stone age tools had a much more pervasive presence in Delhi and
its environs.

[7] Dilip K. Chakrabarti and Nayanjot Lahiri, 'A Preliminary Report on the Stone Age of the
    Union Territory of Delhi and Haryana,' *Man and Environment* 11 (1987): 109–16.

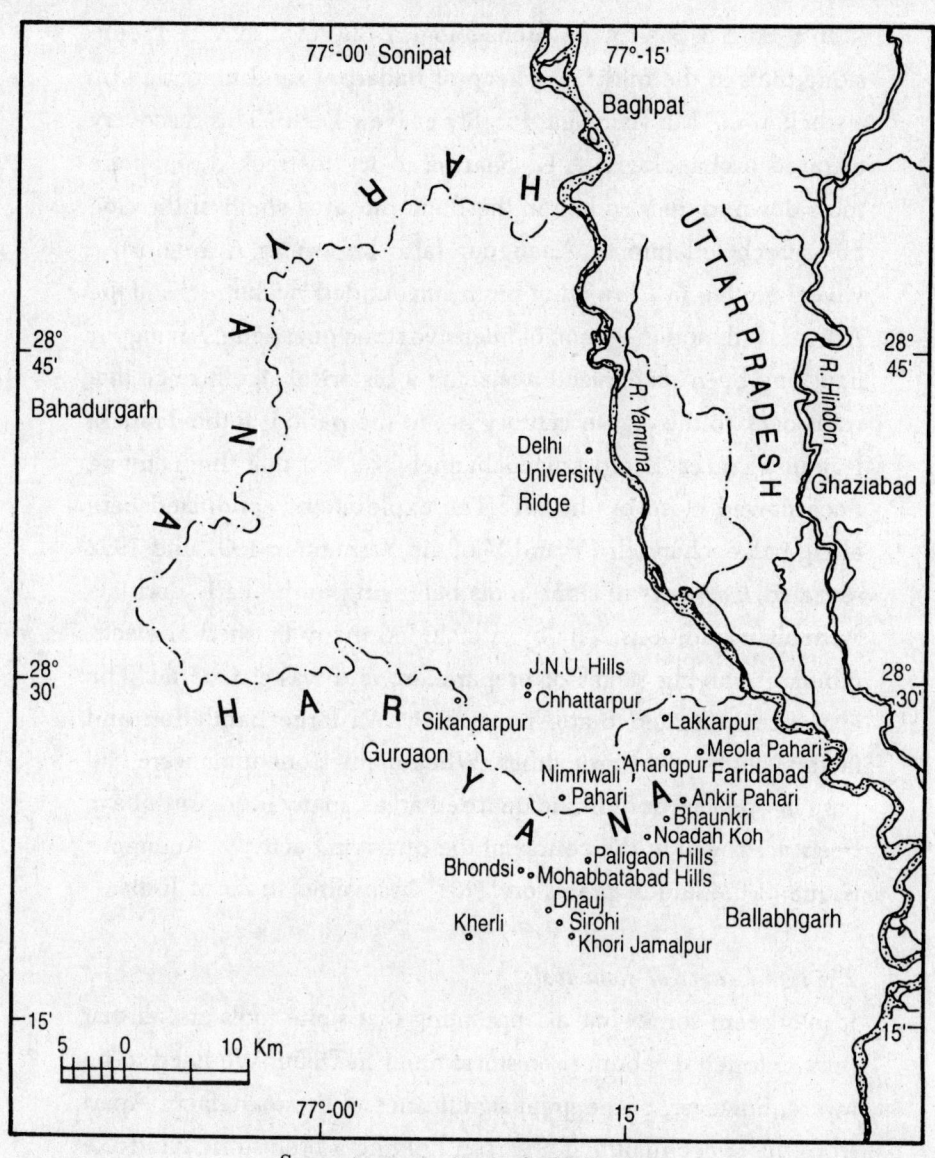

77°-00' Sonipat
77°-15'
Baghpat
H A R Y A N A
UTTAR PRADESH
28° 45'
Bahadurgarh
R. Yamuna
R. Hindon
Delhi University Ridge
Ghaziabad
28° 45'
28° 30'
J.N.U. Hills
Chhattarpur
Lakkarpur
Sikandarpur
Meola Pahari
H A R
Gurgaon
Nimriwali
Anangpur
Faridabad
Y A N A
Pahari
Ankir Pahari
Bhaunkri
Noadah Koh
Paligaon Hills
Bhondsi
Mohabbatabad Hills
Dhauj
Kherli
Sirohi
Ballabhgarh
Khori Jamalpur
28° 30'
-15'
5   0   10 Km
77°-00'
15'
-15'

Some stone age sites in the Delhi area

In 1986, S.S. Saar of the Archaeological Survey discovered some
stone tools in the midst of a heap of Badarpur sand unloaded by
a truck in the Malviyanagar locality of New Delhi. This discovery
inspired archaeologist A.K. Sharma to try to track these stone
tools down to their source in the Badarpur area south of the city.
His search led him to Anangpur (also known as Arangpur), a
village nestled in a low-lying basin surrounded by the rocks of the
Aravalli hills and the scene of intensive stone quarrying. Anangpur
had long been recognized as having a historical significance that
went back to the eighth century AD, to the period of the Tomara
Rajputs. Traces of old palaeochannels showed that the Yamuna
once flowed close by the site. The explorations conducted here
along palaeochannels IV and V of the Yamuna in 1991 and 1992
revealed *thousands* of stone tools belonging to the early and late
Acheulian traditions. The tools included many finished artefacts,
others in varying stages of preparation, and waste material. The
evidence indicated that Anangpur was a large habitation and
factory site in prehistoric times. While many stone tools were laid
bare in open sections in the quarried areas, many more must have
been destroyed in the course of the quarrying activity. Anangpur
is one of the largest prehistoric sites discovered so far in India.

The significance of stone tools

It may seem somewhat disappointing that stone tools are all that
remain to tell us about prehistoric times in Delhi. We need to be
aware, however, of the great significance of these artefacts. Apart
from the excitement that a person holding a prehistoric hand-axe
in his or her hand may feel at the thought that this very object was
held and used by some unknown Delhiite many thousands of
years ago, there are a few other things that we should keep in
mind. The first is that stone tools represent a very important aspect

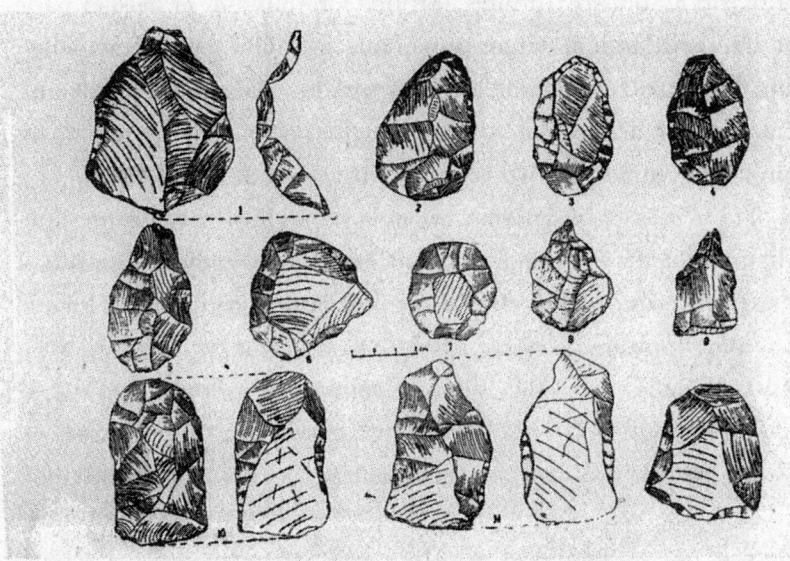

Some stone age tools found in the Delhi area
Courtesy: D.K. Chakrabarti and N. Lahiri

of the life of prehistoric men and women. Although these people used other raw materials such as wood and bone to make tools, stone was the most important raw material which they worked and used. Stone tools therefore represent one of the major ways in which these people interacted with their environment and obtained food for survival. The great range of stone tools, differing from one another in shape, size, and technique, indicates that over the generations, stone age communities developed an impressive repertoire of skills in putting stone to a variety of uses.

A particular stone tool may have had a specific use or may have been a multi-purpose tool. We can sometimes tell by looking at its shape and size what sorts of activities it might have been used for—whether for digging roots, piercing and cutting fruits, slicing meat, or as part of a spear to hunt game. Some archaeologists have tried to understand the uses and techniques of making prehistoric stone tools by turning to tribal communities in certain parts of the world among whom stone tools are still a part of every-day life. Of course, we cannot know for sure to what extent the picture that we get from such studies matches what was going on in prehistoric times, but we certainly do get some useful clues.

The evidence of prehistoric stone tools forces us to question the popular stereotype of stone age humans as brutish, dim-witted creatures, who spent their time lumbering around the place, grunting foolishly. Making stone tools required intelligence, skill, and patience. The skills were developed, no doubt, through a series of trials and errors, but once perfected, were passed on within generations and between generations. Such a transmission of expertise was vital for the survival of stone age people. Because *we* are not the inheritors of such a tradition of expertise, it would be very difficult for us to make even a simple stone tool. Apart from the passing on of knowledge related to tool-making, which has certain important social implications, stone age people must also have cooperated with each other in various activities such as hunting, especially big game hunting. This kind of cooperation would not have been possible unless they could communicate with one another through language. Unfortunately, what *sort* of language prehistoric humans in Delhi or elsewhere spoke, we will never know.

So far, we do not have any prehistoric artistic remains from the Delhi region, but evidence of paintings, etchings, and figurines from other parts of India and the world clearly show that stone age people had fine aesthetic sensibilities and skills, and suggest that prehistoric art was closely linked with some sort of magico-religious beliefs and practices, the details of which elude us.

3

In the Shadow of the First Cities

While stone tools are our prime informants on life in the stone age, pottery takes over this role for the later periods. Like stone tools, pottery was an item of everyday use. Because of this, whatever else may or may not be found in the course of an archaeological exploration or excavation, pottery invariably turns up, often in large quantities. And just as stone tools of different types help archaeologists classify stone age cultures into different categories and phases, similarly, pottery helps to place, identify, and associate the evidence from various archaeological sites. Pots, like stone tools, represent certain ways of making things, and the way people make things is an important part of their culture. The word 'culture' here can be understood in the narrow, technical, archaeological sense of a recurring assemblage of material traits, or in a broader sense as the totality of the way of life of a group of people.

Archaeologists have identified certain types of pottery with certain cultures, geographical regions, and periods of time. Although the interpretation of continuities and changes in ceramic traditions raises a complex series of questions, for certain segments of the most ancient past, pottery does serve as a useful marker of broad cultural phases. For our purposes, Late Harappan pottery, Painted Grey Ware (PGW), and Northern Black Polished Ware (NBPW) are some of the pottery types on the basis of which evidence from settlements ranging from the second millennium BC. to around the beginning of the Christian era can be classified and discussed.

Civilization made its appearance in the Indian subcontinent in the third millennium BC. This civilization is known as the Indus or the Harappan civilization (after the site of Harappa on banks of the Ravi, discovered by Daya Ram Sahni in 1921). Excavations over many decades have shown that this civilization was not confined to the valleys of the river Indus and its tributaries. Other areas that fell within the Harappan culture zone included Rajasthan, Gujarat, northern Maharashtra, Punjab, Haryana, and western Uttar Pradesh. The Harappan civilization did not appear suddenly out of nowhere. It was the outcome of many centuries, even millennia, of cultural development. Neither was it static or unchanging. It was a cultural process in which three interrelated phases can be identified: the early, mature, and the late phases. Today, close to a thousand sites of these three phases taken together have been identified.

While the large cities of the Harappan civilization collapsed by the beginning of the second millennium BC, there is plenty of evidence of the survival of village settlements that formed part of or devolved from it. These Late Harappan settlements had some similarities (for instance in pottery) with the mature, urban phase, minus certain things such as cities and writing.[8] There are regional

---

[8] Archaeological evidence does not support the immensely popular theory of a sudden cataclysmic end of the Harappan civilization due to a terrible massacre of the Harappans by the Vedic Aryans (whoever *they* might have been). It may also be noted that while evidence from the Late Harappan phase at various sites certainly shows that city-life gradually came to an end, it also shows a steady increase in the varieties of crops grown by rural commmunities.

variations in the pottery of the Late Harappan (or post-urban) phase. It is, however, generally wheel-made, medium in fabric (thickness), and is treated with a light or dull red slip (coating). Some pots have incised designs, others have linear, geometric, or naturalistic patterns painted on, usually in black. Compared to the Mature Harappan pottery, the slip of Late Harappan pottery is less bright and the shapes of the pots tend to be thicker and sturdier. Some of the classical Harappan shapes (such as the beaker, goblet, perforated jar, s-shaped and pyriform jar) disappear, while others, such as jars of different shapes, vases, and the dish-on-stand continue in the Late Harappan phase.

Radio-carbon dates for Late Harappan sites are few and far between, and indicate that not all of them were contemporaneous, but the rough time bracket for this phase is *c.* 2000–1000 BC. Late Harappan remains have been found in and around Delhi at the sites of Mandoli, Bhorgarh, Kharkhari-Nahar, and Nachauli.[9] The discoveries at Mandoli and Bhorgarh are particularly significant and spectacular.

Mandoli is a small village on the left bank of the Yamuna near Nand Nagari in east Delhi. There is a mound to the south-west of the village where the Department of Archaeology of the Government of Delhi carried out explorations in 1987–8 and 1988–9.[10] The explorations revealed that the site was occupied from Late Harappan times (the second millennium BC) to the Gupta period (roughly the fourth-fifth centuries AD):

---

[9] See map on p. 44.
[10] For details, *see* B.S.R. Babu, 'Mandoli—A Late Harappan Settlement in Delhi,' in C. Margabandhu and K.S. Ramachandran (eds), *Spectrum of Indian Culture* (Professor S.B. Deo Feliciataion volume) (Delhi: 1996), pp. 98–104.

Table 1: Cultural Sequence[11] at Mandoli

Period V:	Gupta period level
Period IV:	Shunga-Kushana period level
Period III:	A level distinguished by a black-slipped ware
Period II:	Painted Grey Ware level
Break in Occupation	
Period I:	Late Harappan level

The earliest occupation at Mandoli belonged to the Late Harappan phase. The settlement seems to have been fairly small at this stage. No structures survive, but the remains of house floors made of rammed earth and marked with post-holes arranged in a circular and arc pattern were found. The post-holes marked places where wooden posts were erected to support a roof. On one of the mud floors, archaeologists found a burnt terracotta object, and also traces of ash which may indicate that a hearth (used for cooking) was located here. The pottery was wheel-made and included jars with splayed out or beaded rim and vases with disc bases. Some of the pots had a dull red slip (coating). A bead and a circular terracotta cake (the precise use of such 'cakes' is unclear) were also found. The Late Harappan phase of the settlement at Mandoli seems to have come to an end due to floods. This is clear from the pottery, which is worn due to water-logging, and more so from the fact that there is a 30–35 cm. thick layer of

[11] When a site is occupied over a long period of time, archaeologists divide the deposit into a series of periods or phases (and sometimes sub-phases as well). These phases are given a numerical or numerical-cum-alphabetic label. When we refer to an artefact or a structure found at a multi-cultural, i.e. multi-level site, it is essential to mention the stratigraphic context, i.e. to specify in which of the several strata or levels it was found. In terms of age, the archaeological levels that are the deepest are the oldest, and as we move from the lower levels towards the surface of the soil, we move forward in time.

silt and sand over the Late Harappan level, indicating that the site was abandoned for a period of time. The history of Mandoli does not, however, end with its inhabitants fleeing from the flood waters of the Yamuna. We will come back to it later, because it has more to tell us about the ancient history of Delhi.

Late Harappan remains have also been found at Bhorgarh, a village near Narela in north Delhi. The ancient mound here may originally have covered many acres, but over the years almost all of it has been leveled and converted into agricultural fields by villagers. The Yamuna, which today follows a course ten kilometres away from the site, flowed close by in ancient times. The Department of Archaeology of the Government of Delhi excavated Bhorgarh in 1992–3 and 1993–4 under the direction of B.S.R.

The Bhorgarh mound
Courtesy: Department of Archaeology, Government of Delhi

Babu.[12] The excavations revealed that the site was under occupation from the Late Harappan phase right down to the medieval period, a span of some 2,500 years.

Table 2: Cultural sequence at Bhorgarh[13]

Period IV:	Medieval (16th-17th centuries)
Period III:	Kushana (2nd-3rd centuries AD)
Period II:	Painted Grey Ware level (1st millennium BC)
Period I:	Late Harappan (2nd millennium BC)

The earliest phase of the settlement at Bhorgarh yielded fragments of a thick red type of pottery. Archaeologists were not able to find any house remains of this Late Harappan phase, but they did find some graves, one of which contained grave goods in the form of three pots. Grave goods are an indicator of some sort of belief in afterlife; of course the evidence tells us nothing about the precise nature or details of these beliefs. As is the case with Mandoli, we will return to Bhorgarh as we trace the history of Delhi through later ages.

There is a village called Nachauli in the Faridabad district, not far from the old Faridabad bridge.[14] To the south and south-east of this village, there are the remains of an old mound, today cut through, levelled, and converted into agricultural fields. Fragments of Late Harappan pottery and terracotta cakes were found here as surface finds. This area is locally known as *Gauravon ka khera*

---

[12] B.S.R. Babu, 'Excavations at Bhorgarh,' *Puratattva* 25 (1994–5): 88–93.

[13] B.R. Mani suggests that the site may have been inhabited during the Maurya–Shunga period and in the early medieval period as well.

[14] These and all other details of sites in Faridabad are based on the author's joint field-work with N. Lahiri and T. Uberoi. *See* N. Lahiri, Upinder Singh, and Tarika Uberoi, 'Preliminary Field Report on the Archaeology of Faridabad—the Ballabgarh Tehsil,' *Man and Environment,* 21 (1996), 32–57.

(*khera* is a word used frequently for mound in the Delhi area). The 1883–4 *Gazetteer of the Delhi District* quotes a tradition current in the Ballabgarh area that the Gauravas were 'quarrelsome' and 'degenerate' Rajputs. Today, the villagers of Nachauli have no clear recollection of who the Gauravas might have been.

Bhorgarh: Late Harappan burial
Courtesy: Department of Archaeology, Government of India

Late Harappan pottery has also been reported from Kharkhari-Nahar village (near Najafgarh in west Delhi). The discoveries at Mandoli, Bhorgarh, Nachauli, and Kharkhari-Nahar tell us a little about early proto-historic settlements in the Delhi region. We do not know the names of the people who lived here, nor do we know anything about the events that they experienced as individuals or as communities. What we do get are a few, tangible fragments of the things their every day life was made of.

4

Fragments of Pottery and
the Great War

In the history of north India, the half-century between c. 1000 BC and 500 BC was the period during which later Vedic literature—which includes the later hymns of the *Rig Veda*, the *Sama, Yajur,* and *Atharva Vedas,* the *Brahmanas, Aranyakas,* and *Upanishads*—is supposed to have been composed.[15] The geographical area with which these texts were familiar included the *doab* region (the land between the Ganga and Yamuna rivers) and the middle-Ganga valley. The Vedic texts contain a variety of religious, philosophical and liturgical matter. Indirect references to mundane aspects of life embedded in the midst of all this esoteric material suggest that this was an age when society in this part of north India was gradually making the transition from a tribal, lineage-based system to a more complex one in which social classes were emerging and state structures evolving.

The city of Indraprastha

Delhi steps into the glare of power politics for the first time in the age of the great Indian epic the *Mahabharata,* when Yudhishthira

---

[15] Although this time-bracket can be accepted for the sake of convenience, in view of the enormous difficulties in dating Vedic literature, all such chronologies must be taken as approximate.

and his brothers are depicted as founding the city of Indraprastha on the banks of the Yamuna. Before proceeding to look at what the epic says about Indraprastha and what archaeologists discovered in the course of excavations at the Purana Qila (Old Fort), it is necessary to pose and try to answer certain questions about the text and the story of the *Mahabharata*: When was the epic composed and compiled? Do we know the identity of its author or authors? Did the events mentioned in the epic—especially the great war between the Pandavas and Kauravas—ever happen, or do they fall within the realm of mythology? If these events *did* happen, when might that have been?

The *Mahabharata* is an extremely voluminous text, with an enormous range in theme and content. Of course, there *is* a central plot—the story of two feuding factions of the Bharata people fighting for control over Kurukshetra (the land of the Kurus), which included the modern Thaneswar, Delhi and upper Gangetic *doab* regions. But there is much in the *Mahabharata* that has at the most very tenuous links with the main story-line. Stories within stories, discourses on the many aspects of *dharma* (righteous conduct), and religious teaching blend together in such a manner that, as van Buitenan remarks, what we have is not so much one work but 'a library of opera'.[16] According to tradition, Krishna Dvaipayana Vyasa was the author of the *Mahabharata*. But the present form of the text (consisting of some 100,000 verses) cannot be the work of a single individual, no matter how prodigious a poet he might have been. The epic clearly spans many ages, and its composition may be placed approximately during the period *c.* 500 BC–500 AD.

---

[16] For a good, but unfortunately incomplete English translation of the *Mahabharata, see* the volumes translated and edited by J.A.B. van Buitenan and published by the University of Chicago Press. There is the older eleven-volume P.C. Roy translation (the actual translator was K.M. Ganguli), *as also* P. Lal's rendering of the epic.

It was orally transmitted for much of this period, towards the end of which it was compiled. Many historians agree that the *Mahabharata* epic may be based on certain historical events that might have happened some time around 1000 BC. Of course there is no definite *proof* for this. We are talking about the realm of possibility, or at the most, probability.

We catch up with the story of the *Mahabharata* at the point when the Pandavas appear in the court of their uncle King Dhritarashtra, demanding their share of the kingdom. They arrive in Hastinapura after many adventures during exile, having survived their cousin Duryodhana's attempt to have them burnt to death in a house of lac. They are accompanied by their mother Kunti and their wife, the beautiful Panchala princess Draupadi, won by Arjuna in an archery contest. The Pandavas are greeted joyously by the people of Hastinapura. Dhritarashtra persuades them to avoid conflict with their Kaurava cousins and to accept half the kingdom. The Pandavas agree and the kingdom is divided, the Kauravas continuing to rule from Hastinapura on the banks of the Ganga, the Pandavas establishing themselves in the forested Khandava tract, which included the Delhi region. This episode is recounted towards the end of the *Adi Parva*, the first book of the *Mahabharata*.

In the Khandava forest, the epic tells us, the Pandavas founded Indraprastha, a city as beautiful as a new heaven. The brothers performed the appropriate rites and built a fort surrounded by an ocean-like moat. The fort had massive walls and huge double-hung gates with imposing towers, covered with many kinds of spears and javelins. The city itself is described as being resplendent with well-planned streets, magnificent white buildings, pavilions, pleasure hillocks, ponds, lakes, and tanks. It was surrounded by beautiful gardens where trees of many kinds blossomed and bore fruit and where the air resounded with the call of peacocks and cuckoos. Learned Brahmins, merchants from many regions, artisans skilled in every craft sought their abode in Indraprastha. From here, Yudhishthira ruled over his realm, cultivating among his subjects *dharma* (righteousness and spiritual well-being), *artha* (material well-being), and *kama* (the satisfaction of sensual pleasure).[17]

An important episode connected with the Pandavas' settling the Khandava tract and establishing their kingdom and capital city is the burning of the Khandava forest. In the sequence of the epic's narrative, it occurs at the end of the *Adi Parva*, after the events mentioned above. This violent incident has an innocuous enough prelude, with Arjuna suggesting to Krishna that they go to the banks of the Yamuna for fun and frolic. The mood of drunken revelry is disturbed by the appearance of the fire god Agni in the form of a Brahmin. Agni asks Arjuna and Krishna to help him burn down the Khandava forest. The epic then describes the conflagration that engulfs the forest and the ruthless and systematic destruction of virtually all the animals, birds, fish—the creatures to whom the forest was home—by Agni, Krishna, and Arjuna. The mood is one of exultation as the three ruthlessly kill the terrified, fleeing creatures of the forest, and thwart the god Indra's attempt to end the massacre. The epic tells us that so horrendous was the spectacle that when the gods found themselves helpless in interceding, they turned their faces away. In the end, only six creatures survived the fire—Ashvasena, (son of the serpent king Takshaka), a *danava* (demon) named Maya, and four *Sharngaka* birds. Agni offered Arjuna and Krishna boons in recompense for their assistance. Arjuna obtained all sorts of magnificent weapons,

---

[17] *Dharma, artha,* and *kama* are the *purusharthas*—the legitimate goals of human existence—recognized in the classical Brahmanical tradition. Some texts list a fourth *purushartha*—*moksha* (liberation from the cycle of birth, death, and rebirth).

and Krishna his desire for eternal friendship with Arjuna. The violent episode ends on a serene note with Arjuna, Krishna, and Maya sitting down together on the banks of the Yamuna.

Apart from the fact that it shows Krishna and Arjuna behaving in an uncharacteristically ruthless and cruel fashion, the burning of the Khandava forest as an episode has been interpreted allegorically by historians. Connections have been made between fire and the ritual consecration of territory. Further, the episode suggests to us how the inhospitable forested Khandava tract (of which the Delhi region was a part) was brought under habitation and cultivation in ancient times—by burning.

Another *Mahabharata* episode relevant to the ancient history of Delhi, and one that is more specifically connected with Indraprastha, occurs in the beginning of the *Sabha Parva*, the second book of the epic. Maya, one of the few fortunate survivors of the forest fire mentioned above, wants to express his thanks to Arjuna, due to whose compassion he had escaped death. Maya, it turns out, is no ordinary demon but a talented architect. Krishna suggests to him that he build a magnificent assembly hall in the city of Indraprastha, one that would defy emulation and excite admiration the world over. The epic tells us that Maya proceeded to build a wonderful golden-pillared hall, studded with precious stones, ten thousand cubits in circumference. Inside the hall was an exquisitely clear lotus pond, filled with lotuses, turtles, fish, and aquatic fowl. The *Mahabharata* tells us that some kings who came here did not realize it was a pond and tumbled into it. When the great sage Narada arrived in the hall, Yudhishthira anxiously asked him whether he had ever seen an assembly hall such as his. Narada replied that he had neither seen nor heard of such a hall in the world of men. Of course, the halls in the world of the gods were another matter.

Indraprastha is thus an important place in the *Mahabharata* narrative. The extravagant poetic descriptions of the city, however, are designed to impress rather than to provide historically accurate information. And since the composition of the *Mahabharata* seems to have spanned a thousand years or so, the descriptions of cities and palaces in the epic do not—in fact *cannot*—reflect the nature of settlements at the time when the Pandavas and Kauravas may have fought out their bloody feud. Archaeological evidence shows that cities simply did not exist in India in around 1000 BC. The 'urbanity' of the epic was obviously a later superimposition on the story, and belongs to a later stage in its evolution.

Excavations at the Purana Qila

We turn from literature to archaeology. What exactly did archaeologists discover at the site of the Purana Qila, the sixteenth century fort built by Humayun and Sher Shah Sur? How does what was found during the excavations compare with the descriptions of Indraprastha in the *Mahabharata*? One of the problems in answering these questions is that a complete report of the Purana Qila excavations has not been published. What are available are some details of the various seasons of work at the site published in *Indian Archaeology—A Review*, the journal of the Archaeological Survey of India.[18]

A trial excavation was carried out at the Purana Qila in 1954–5 under the direction of B.B. Lal. The aim was to find out how old the site was and whether it could be identified with Indraprastha of the *Mahabharata* legend. The discovery of sherds of Painted Grey Ware (the time-frame for which is roughly 1000–500 BC)[19]

---

[18] *Indian Archaeology—A Review*, 1994–5, 1969–70, 1970–1.
[19] There is some difference of opinion among archaeologists about the chronology of the Painted Grey Ware Phase.

Painted Grey Ware sherds from Mandoli
Courtesy: Department of Archaeology, Government of Delhi

indicated that the settlement might well be as old as about 1000
BC. Painted Grey Ware is a fine grey pottery, thin in fabric. The
pots are often decorated with black designs such as dots-and-dashes,
vertical oblique and criss-cross lines, circles and semi-circles, a
chain of short spirals, sigmas, and *svastikas*.[20] Apart from pottery,
the excavations unearthed artefacts (mostly of copper) such as
sickles and nail-parers. The evidence indicated that the site continued to be occupied till the early centuries AD. As the excavations
could not be completed, a full profile of the site did not emerge.

In 1969–70, an excavation was carried out at the Purana Qila
by a team of archaeologists led by B.B. Lal, B.K. Thapar, and

[20] PGW has been found in Sindh, Punjab, Haryana, north Rajasthan, and western Uttar
Pradesh. It has also been found in north Bihar and in Madhya Pradesh. It should be
pointed out that PGW is a *de luxe* ware and that it does not comprise more than 10% of
the total pottery find at sties where it has been found. Other pottery types found at
PGW levels include black-and-red ware, black-slipped ware, and red and grey wares.

The Purana Qila excavations in progress. Courtesy: Archaeological Survey of India

M.C. Joshi. This excavation gave some more information on the cultural sequence of the site and also tried to lay bare portions of the settlements of various levels. Remains of periods ranging from the Northern Black Polished Ware (NBPW) levels of around the fourth/third centuries BC up to the medieval period were unearthed.

Table 3: Cultural sequence at the Purana Qila

Period VIII:	Mughal period (16th–19th century)
Period VII:	Sultanate period (13th–15th century)
Period VI:	Rajput period (10th–12th century)
Period V:	post-Gupta period (7th–9th century)
Period IV:	Gupta period (4th–6th century)
Period III:	Shaka-Kushana period (1st–3rd century AD)
Period II:	Shunga period (2nd–1st century BC)
Period I:	Northern Black Polished Ware level (4th–3rd century BC)

(PGW sherds found, but PGW level not identified)

Excavations were resumed at the Purana Qila in 1970–1, this time with the dual aim of exposing the pre-Mauryan (pre-fourth century B.C.) strata including the Painted Grey Ware level, and of laying bare larger areas. Three trial trenches were dug at different spots to try to find the Painted Grey Ware level, but to no avail. The excavation confirmed the already established cultural sequence from the Northern Black Polished Ware (NBPW) levels up to the Mughal period.

The details of the earliest phases of settlement at the site of the Purana Qila are thus disappointingly meagre. Although a regular PGW level was not located in any of the excavations, the discovery of sherds of this pottery indicated that such a level must have been located somewhere nearby. The PGW sherds also suggest that the antiquity of the Purana Qila site goes back a long way, perhaps to around 1000 BC. Far from the discovery of anything resembling the epic details of the city of Indraprastha, its fortifications, residences, palaces, and the magnificent hall that Maya designed, *no* structural remains of this earliest period were found. There is, of course, always the possibility that future excavations at the site may reveal something more or something new.

Excavations at the Purana Qila and other sites connected with the *Mahabharata* story—such as Hastinapura, Panipat, Baghpat, Kurukshetra, etc. where PGW has also been found—neither prove nor disprove the historicity of the *Mahabharata* events. What they *do* show is that these sites were inhabited from ancient times, perhaps from around 1000 BC and that people living here shared a broadly similar sort of material culture.

The link between the Purana Qila and ancient Indraprastha
If nothing *specifically* connected with the *Mahabharata* events was found at the Purana Qila, on what basis is this site identified with Indraprastha of the great epic? The answer lies in local traditions, the earliest written accounts of which belong to the medieval period. Writing in the sixteenth century during the reign of the Mughal emperor Akbar, Abul Fazl gives in his *Ain-i-Akbari* a synopsis of the *Mahabharata* events. He states that Delhi, one of the greatest cities of antiquity, was first called Indrapat. He goes on to say that the emperor Humayun restored the citadel of Indrapat and named it Dinpanah (literally, 'Asylum of the Faith'). There is a reference in Shams Siraj Afif's fourteenth century work the *Tarikh-i Firuz Shahi* to Indraprastha being the headquarters of a *pargana* (district). A fourteenth century stone inscription found at Naraina village in

west Delhi speaks of Nadayana (i.e. Naraina) village being situated
to the west of Indraprastha. Abul Fazl's statements indicate that in
the sixteenth century, there was a strong tradition connecting the
Pandava capital of Indraprastha with the site of the Purana Qila,
where Humayan's Dinpanah was situated. Furthermore, till the
end of the nineteenth century there was actually a village called
Indarpat located within the walls of the Old Fort.

Local traditions and legends claim a few more epic connections
for Delhi. One of these holds Nigambodh on the banks of the
Yamuna to be the place where Yudhishthira poured the oblations
into the sacrificial fire after performing the *ashvamedha*, the 'horse
sacrifice' which signified political paramountcy. Not far from
Nigambodh is the Nili Chhatri temple. According to local tradition,
Yudhishthira built a temple here. The present structure is of a late
date, but there is a possiblility that it marks the site of an older
shrine.

Indraprastha seems to have faded in importance in the post-
Mahabharata war period. There is a tradition that speaks of the
Pandavas ruling at Indraprastha for thirty-six years. It tells us that
one day a fly fell into Yudhishthira's food and, interpreting this as
a bad omen, he transferred his court to Hastinapura, leaving
Indraprastha in the hands of the only surviving son of
Dhritarashtra.[21] The *Vishnu Purana* tells of a shift of the capital
from Hastinapur to Kaushambi due to a massive flood in the Ganga
during the reign of king Nichakshu, fifth king after Parikshit.[22]
This too suggests that the capital had at some previous point in
time moved from Indraprastha to Hastinapura. Indraprastha is
mentioned in the Buddhist *Jataka* tales as the capital of a line of

[21] This was Yuyutsu, son of Dhritarashtra by a concubine.
[22] Parikshit was the son of Abhimanyu and grandson of Arjuna. It was he who became king
after the *Mahabharata* war.

kings claiming to belong to the 'Yudhitthila gotra' (Yudhishthira's clan).[23] Putting together these sorts of references (the historicity of many of which is suspect), we do get a general sense of Indraprastha's decline during the reigns of Yudhishthira's successors. Hastinapur regained its place as the political centre of the Kurus.

The region of Kurukshetra soon lost its political importance and the centre of political gravity in north India shifted to regions lying further east. But the name of Indraprastha lived on as the name of an administrative unit till medieval times.

Tilpat, Sihi, and Bisrakh

We have noted the discovery of sherds of PGW in the Purana Qila excavations. This type of pottery has been found elsewhere in the Delhi area as well, usually in the form of surface finds, occasionally in the course of a regular excavation, revealing evidence of periods of occupation ranging roughly from c. 1000-500 BC. Some of these PGW sites are connected with epic legends, either in the great Sanskritic or local tradition, others are not.

The village of Tilpat is situated about 1.8 km. east of the Delhi-Agra highway in the Faridabad district. The village lies atop a mound that rises steeply to a height of about 30 m. and covers an area of some 4–5 hectares. Archaeology and literary tradition indicate that it has a history that goes back to a very early period. Tilpat has been identified with the village of Tilaprastha mentioned in the *Mahabharata* epic as one of the five villages demanded by the Pandavas as part of their share of the kingdom. A small-scale excavation was carried out here in the 1950s and B.B. Lal reported the discovery of PGW and NBPW levels, confirming the antiquity of the site.

---

[23] The *Jatakas* are tales of the previous lives of the Buddha. They form a later part of the *Tripitaka*, the Pali canon. The period of composition of the Jatakas can be placed roughly between the third century B.C. and the second century A.D.

Sihi village lies opposite Sector 7 in the heart of residential Faridabad. There is an approximately 10 m. high mound at the periphery of the village, on top of which is perched a Government Boys' Primary School. Painted Grey Ware has been found on this mound, suggesting its antiquity. But Sihi has dramatic credentials apart from this. A plaque in the school informs the visitor that this is the birthplace of the famous late fifteenth/early sixteenth century devotional poet Surdas.[24] Even more intriguing is the local tradition that holds this to be the place where king Janamejaya performed his great snake sacrifice.

The snake sacrifice was the occasion on which the *Mahabharata* is supposed to have been narrated to king Janamejaya by the sage Vaishampayana. Janamejaya was the son of Parikshit (who became king after the *Mahabharata* war). Pariskshit died due to a snake-bite and Janamejaya decided to avenge his father's death by performing a sacrifice which would destroy all the snakes in the world. Janamejaya's snake sacrifice has been interpreted by some historians as an allegory of the conflict between brahmanical culture and certain culturally different, non-Aryan peoples known as Nagas (*naga* means snake).

The *Adi Parva* of the *Mahabharata* gives a graphic account of the sacrifice and describes how millions of snakes, irresistibly drawn to the sacrificial fire, came hissing, writhing, and screaming through the air, and fell into the sacrificial fire as the priests chanted the verses and poured in the oblations. The sacrifice did not, however, succeed in its aim. Many snakes perished but not all did. Takshaka, the serpent king, who had escaped from the forest fire that engulfed the Khandava forest by being absent from the scene, escaped

---

[24] The *Bhavaprakasha Tika* on the *Chaurasi Vaishnavan ki Varta* by Harilal, written about a hundred years after the demise of Surdas, states that the poet was born in Sihi, 4 *kos* away from Dilli. While this testimony is accepted by most scholars, some hold that Surdas was born in Runkuta in Agra district, U.P.

once again. He sought refuge with the god Indra, but was ultimately saved by Astika, a Brahmin of serpentine descent. Picture the dramatic scene: Astika rushes into the sacrificial arena to prevent the extermination of his kinsfolk. As Takshaka falls from the heavens from the hands of the god Indra, unconscious with the terror of impending death, Astika says the word 'Stay' three times. The snake king, suspended at that moment between heaven and earth, is saved in the nick of time. Janamejaya has already agreed to grant a boon to Astika and now the brahmin expresses his desire that the sacrifice be terminated. Naturally, the king has to honour his promise and so the sacrifice comes to a premature end.

According to the *Mahabharata*, the snake sacrifice of Janamejaya took place at Takshashila (i.e. Taxila, 20 miles north-west of Rawalpindi in Pakistan). Yet the inhabitants of Sihi village in Faridabad will tell you that the great snake sacrifice happened in *their* village. One of the interesting aspects of the Sihi mound is that large quantities of old iron slag (the waste product of iron smelting) have been found and continue to be found here. According to local tradition, these fragments of iron slag are the remains of the bones of snakes that perished long ago in Janamejaya's sacrifice. Practitioners of traditional medicine from as afar as Meerut believe this slag to have miraculous healing properties, particularly as an antidote for poison. A truly remarkable series of associations link together a major epic event, the mundane remains of metal crafting, and traditional medicinal practice. Equally remarkable is how local tradition has plucked out an event from the *Mahabharata* epic and planted it here in Sihi village.

We see another example of local tradition taking over an epic event in the village of Bisrakh in the Ghaziabad district of Uttar Pradesh. The village is situated on a high mound. Like Tilpat and

Sihi, Bisrakh too is a place where PGW has been found. This establishes its ancient credentials. While Tilpat and Sihi either had or came to acquire connections with the *Mahabharata* legend, local tradition links Bisrakh with the other great Sanskrit epic, the *Ramayana*. According to this tradition, Ravana, the king of Lanka, the abductor of Sita and the overall chief villain of the Ramayana, was born here, in Bisrakh. There are a number of medieval Shiva *lingas* (phallic emblems, the most popular form in which the god Shiva is worshipped) in various parts of the village and also a headless sculpture of the Nandi bull, the vehicle of Shiva. This ties in very neatly with the fact that Ravana is supposed to have been an ardent worshipper of Shiva. All this is presented by the villagers of Bisrakh as 'proof' that their village is in fact the place where Ravana was born.

Shiva *lingas* and Nandi bull at Bisrakh
Photograph: N. Lahiri

1 The Yamuna near Okhla
Photograph: Ravi Agarwal

2 The rocky hill-side at Dhauj
Photograph: N. Lahiri

3 The Ridge forest
Photograph: Ravi Agarwal

4 Late Harappan vase; Bhorgarh
Courtesy: Department of Archaeology,
Government of Delhi

5 Late Harappan bowl; Bhorgarh
Courtesy: Department of Archaeology,
Government of Delhi

6 Painted Grey Ware dish; Mandoli
Courtesy: Department of Archaeology, Government of Delhi

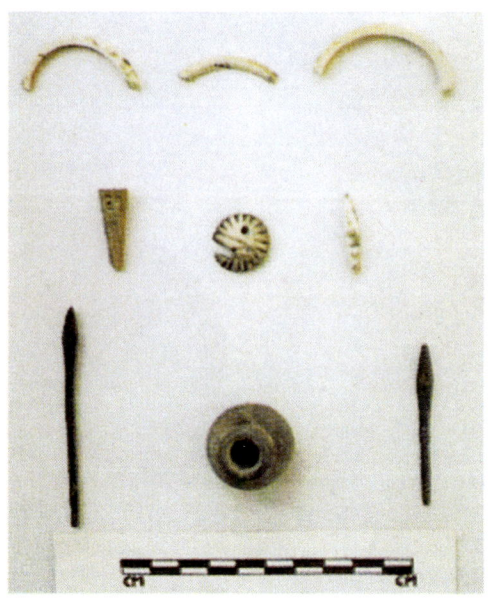

7 Ornaments and other artefacts, PGW level; Mandoli
Courtesy: Department of Archaeology, Government of Delhi

8 Fragments of moulded pottery: early centuries A.D.; Mandoli
Courtesy: Department of Archaeology, Government of Delhi

9 The Bahapur rocks
Photograph: Author

10 The Delhi–Topra pillar
Photograph: V. Tankha

11 The Delhi–Meerut pillar
Photograph: V. Tankha

12 The ascent of the Tilpat mound
Photograph: N. Lahiri

13 Village shrine; Tilpat
Photograph: N. Lahiri

14 Nachauli: section of the mound
Photograph: N. Lahiri

15 Ancient Shiva *linga* in the
midst of fields; Nachauli
Photograph: N. Lahiri

16 The Mehrauli iron pillar
Photograph: Aditya Arya

17 Pillars of the Qutb mosque
Photograph: Aditya Arya

उ०३ नवाण प्रथ्वीराजजी ने चंद भाट   ३७

18 Painting of Prithviraja Chauhan with poet Chand Bardai; Jodhpur Style
Courtesy: National Museum

19 The Suraj Kund reservoir
Photograph: Aditya Arya

20 The dam at Anangpur
Photograph: Aditya Arya

While Tilpat is a case of a modern village which marks an ancient site mentioned in the epic tradition, Sihi and Bisrakh are instances of villages with a long history in the neighbourhood of Delhi which have blithely borrowed (hijacked, so to speak) an event and an association from the epic tradition. How and when this borrowing took place is something which we do not know. But it is interesting that in both cases, the villages in question are not upstart modern villages but ones which the pottery remains prove to be very old, going back perhaps to around 1000 BC. Sihi and Bisrakh are therefore important parts of the ancient history of the Delhi region in their own right.

Other Painted Grey Ware sites
Painted Grey Ware has been discovered at Bhorgarh and Mandoli, mentioned earlier as villages where Late Harappan pottery was found. In Period II at Bhorgarh, post-holes in the excavated sections suggest that people lived in roundish huts supported by wooden posts. A clay hearth, carnelian and clay beads, terracotta animal figurines, hop scotches (terracotta pieces the use of which we are not sure about), and fragments of iron implements are among the other remains of the first millennium BC. At Mandoli, there is a break in occupation between Period I (Late Harappan) and Period II (PGW), showing that the site was deserted for some time and then reoccupied. At PGW levels archaeologists found remains of houses in the form of rammed-mud floors and post holes. The finds included terracotta animal figurines, agate and carnelian beads, an antimony rod, copper nail parer, and iron slag.

A number of other sites in and around Delhi have given evidence of PGW. These include Kharkhari Nahar and Jhatikra (near Najafgarh), Salimgarh (near the Red Fort), Majnu-ka-Tila (north of Kashmiri Gate), Gordon Highlanders Column (near Badli-ki-

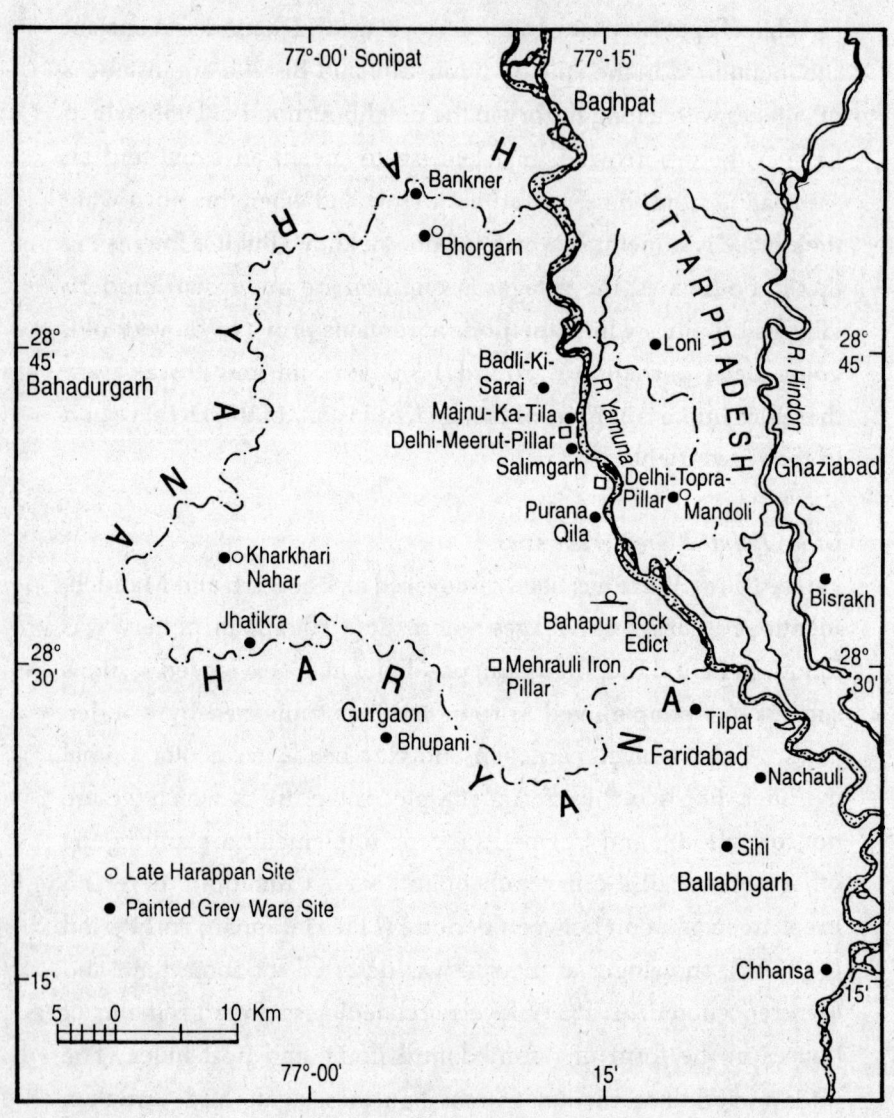

Early sites in the Delhi area

Sarai village), Bankner (near Bhorgarh), Loni (in Ghaziabad district), Bhupani and Chhansa (these last two are in the Faridabad district).[25] Two of these sites—Majnu-ka-Tila and Salimgarh—are close to the banks of the Yamuna.

What all this adds up to is that there is evidence of a large number of settlements belonging roughly to the period 1000–500 BC in the Delhi area. Here, as in many other parts of north India, the PGW sites give evidence of the use of iron. We do not have a lot of detail about these settlements—their size, the details of structures, the way of life of the people who lived here. In general, however, the PGW phase appears to have been a phase when the upper and middle Ganga valley was experiencing a prelude to urbanization. Full-fledged urban life and all that it entailed emerged during the next few centuries.

[25] Details of many of these sites can be found in B.R. Mani's 'Excavations at Lal Kot 1991-2 and Further Explorations in Delhi', *Puratattva*, 22 (1991–2) and *Delhi–threshold of the Orient*. For the Faridabad sites, *see* Lahiri, Singh, and Uberoi, 'Preliminary Field Report'.

5

A Tale of Two Pillars

The sixth century BC was an age of political contest and philosophical inquiry. During the sixth to the second centuries BC social, political, and economic processes of the preceding centuries reached maturity. In north India, cities and towns made their appearance. Buddhist texts speak eloquently about flourishing urban life and trade in the Indian subcontinent. Iron became an increasingly important metal and was put to various uses, including the making of agricultural implements. Money made its appearance in the form of silver and copper coins.[26] Society became marked by greater differences in the levels of wealth and status and by the emergence of the institution of caste. From the sixth century BC, our literary sources of historical information—brahmanical, Buddhist, and Jaina texts—become more diverse and eloquent, and the picture of the history of north India grows clearer. There are good reasons to argue that the historical period in India begins in the sixth century BC.

On the political front, our sources speak of sixteen *mahajana-padas* or great states. Most of these were monarchies, a few were

[26] The earliest coins minted in India were square or rectangular strips of metal with various symbols punched on them. Historians and numismatists refer to them as punch-marked coins. In ancient Indian literature they were called *kahapanas* or *karshapanas*.

ganas or non-monarchical states. The *ganas* were not 'republics,' but oligarchies—political systems where power was shared by a group of aristocratic families, unlike the monarchies where it was vested in the hands of a single person, the king. In the sixth century BC, the Delhi region would have formed part of the Kuru kingdom. The Kurus seem to have been allied with the Panchalas, whose principality lay to their east. The Buddhist *Jatakas* refer to Indapatta as the Kuru capital, and describe it as extending over seven leagues. They talk of a chieftain named Koravya ruling the Kuru country in the time of the Buddha. The Jaina *Uttaradhyayana Sutra* refers to a Kuru king named Isukara who ruled from the ancient and prosperous town of Isukara (the town was apparently named after the king). Although counted among the sixteen great states during the age of the Buddha, the Kuru kingdom was not a major player in the power struggles of the time. The details of its history are not clear, but it seems as though the principality came to be parcelled out between two or more lineages. Some time during the post-sixth century BC period, the Kurus seem to have changed over from a monarchical to an oligarchic form of government.

The major political conflicts of this age were fought out among the kingdoms of Kosala, Vatsa, Avanti, and Magadha. By the fourth century BC, Magadha (in south-east Bihar), then ruled by a line of kings belonging to the Nanda dynasty, was the most powerful state in north India. It is difficult to get a precise idea of the dimensions and boundaries of ancient Indian kingdoms and empires. The Nanda kings seem to have carved out a fairly large empire in northern India, including the Kuru and Panchala territory, and perhaps extending southwards into the Deccan. It was on the foundations laid the earlier rulers of Magadha, particularly the Nandas, that the Mauryas carved out a huge empire, extending over almost all of the subcontinent. Pataliputra (identified with modern Patna in Bihar) was the capital of this empire.

The Delhi region formed part of the Magadhan empire under the Nandas and then the Mauryas. Chandragupta (324–300 BC), the first Mauryan king, was probably responsible for the major conquests which led to the creation of an empire extending from the north-western fringes of the subcontinent to the deep south. Chandragupta was succeeded by his son Bindusara (300–272 BC), and Bindusara by his son Ashoka (269–32 BC). Ashoka's fame does not rest on his conquests. (He is known to have launched only one major military campaign during his entire career—against Kalinga in Orissa). It rests on his being an ardent follower and propagator of the Buddhist teaching.

Northern Black Polished Ware levels at the Purana Qila
What do we know about the life of ordinary people in the Delhi area during the early historical period? To answer this question, we turn to the archaeological evidence from NBPW sites. The NBPW is a fine pottery, made of well-levigated clay, generally on a fast wheel. It is thin in fabric and has a dark surface and a strikingly lustrous (almost metallic) sheen. The shapes include dishes, bowls, lids, and carinated *handis* (cooking pots). Like the PGW, NBPW is a *de luxe* pottery, and forms a small percentage of the total pottery yield from levels in which it is found.[27]

It needs to be emphasized that there is no neat 'match' or 'fit' between the pottery-based 'cultures' of archaeology and the dynastic 'periods' of political history. The NBPW culture can be placed within the broad time bracket of the seventh/sixth century

---

[27] The name given to this pottery type is more than a little misleading. It has been found in north India (Uttar Pradesh, Bihar, Rajasthan), but also occurs in other parts of the country (Madhya Pradesh, Maharashtra, and Andhra Pradesh). And while the sheen of this pottery is striking, it is not the result of polishing.

Purana Qila: terracotta ring wells. Courtesy: Archaeological Survey of India

BC to the first century BC. The Mauryan period stretches from the fourth to the second centuries BC. There is thus a partial overlap between the NBPW culture and the Mauryan phase.

Northern Black Polished Ware has been found at several places in and around Delhi, but we have detailed information only from the Purana Qila. These details help in reconstructing every-day life during this phase. The NBPW levels at the Purana Qila indicate that people lived in houses made of both mud-bricks and kiln-made bricks. A burnt wattle-and-daub structure and a series of hearths were found. Houses had drains made of both rectangular and wedge-shaped bricks. Terracotta ring wells (roughly 75 cm. in diameter) were other significant finds of the NBPW level. The technique of making these wells, which may have functioned as soak-pits for waste water, was as follows: first, an oblong pit of the required depth, with a narrow rounded end, was dug in the ground. Terracotta rings were then fitted into it, one on top of the other. The pit was then filled to the brim with rubble and earth.

Terracotta figurines of humans and animals, the fragment of a sculpted ring stone (associated with the worship of the mother goddess), a terracotta piece depicting a horse and armoured rider, a clay sealing with motifs, small rings and an agate disc were also found at the Purana Qila. One of the NBPW dishes bore on its inner base the stamped figure of an elephant. Punch-marked and cast copper coins make their appearance. A terracotta seal which seems to have the inscription 'Svatirakhitasa' (of or belonging to Svatirakhita) and another with 'Seyankarasa' (of or belonging to Seyankara)—were discovered. Who Svatirakhita and Seyankara were, we do not know.

Purana Qila: terracotta figurines of the Mauryan period
Courtesy: Archaeological Survey of India

Ashokan edicts in Delhi

The Mauryan emperor Ashoka had a series of edicts on *dhamma* (the Prakrit form of the Sanskrit word *dharma*) engraved on rocks and pillars in different parts of his empire. This *dhamma* consisted of certain ethical ideals inspired by, but not identical to, those emphasized by early Buddhism.

Most of Ashoka's inscriptions are written in the Prakrit language (akin to Sanskrit and regarded as closer to the everyday speech of the time) and Brahmi script. In the north-western part of his empire, Ashoka used the Kharoshthi script to spread his message. Certain Greek and Aramaic inscriptions, some bilingual and bi-scriptual, have also been found in these parts. Ashoka's inscriptions have a special importance because of their remarkable content and for what they tell us about the king's ideas. They are among the oldest deciphered inscriptions in the Indian subcontinent. Between the decline of the Harappan civilization and the Mauryan period, there are *no* examples of writing found so far in India.[28] What is likely is that people wrote on perishable material such as palm leaves or bark, and that such specimens of writing have simply not survived the ravages of time. When Ashoka Maurya decided to have his edicts inscribed on durable material—stone—he gave later ages the opportunity to read his message. He also left his signature (not literally of course) in places that formed part of his empire. As time passed, the script of the Ashokan inscriptions was forgotten. It was deciphered in 1837 by a scholar named James Prinsep.[29]

Today, there are three places in Delhi where Ashoka's edicts can be seen.[30] A version of Minor Rock Edict I is inscribed on a set of rocks situated at Bahapur, to the south of Srinivaspuri, in south Delhi.[31] There are also two Ashokan pillars in Delhi, one (known as the Delhi–Meerut pillar) on the Delhi Ridge opposite the entrance to Bara Hindu Rao hospital, near the University of Delhi campus, and the second (known as the Delhi–Topra pillar)

[28] It should be pointed out that the Harappan and Brahmi scripts are not related to each other in any way.

[29] The remarkable James Prinsep came to India in 1819 as an assistant to the Assay Master of the Calcutta Mint and soon became a major figure in early-nineteenth-century Indian antiquarian studies. Prinsep was Secretary of the Asiatic Society in Calcutta between 1832 and 1838. The results of his historical, textual, inscriptional, and numismatic research appeared frequently in various volumes of the *Journal of the Asiatic Society of Bengal* and were published posthumously in a collection entitled *Indian Antiquities* (London, 1858). Prinsep's decipherment of Ashokan Brahmi in 1837 was the culmination of the efforts of various other scholars such as Charles Wilkins. Apart from his own prodigious scholarly output, Prinsep was a source of inspiration for many of his contemporaries. James Prinsep and Sir Alexander Cunningham shared a close association, which Cunningham speaks movingly of in the Introduction to the first volume of his *Reports*.

[30] *See* map on p.44.

[31] The rock edict is close to the newly-built gigantic ISKCON temple on Raja Dhir Singh Marg, not far from Nehru Place.

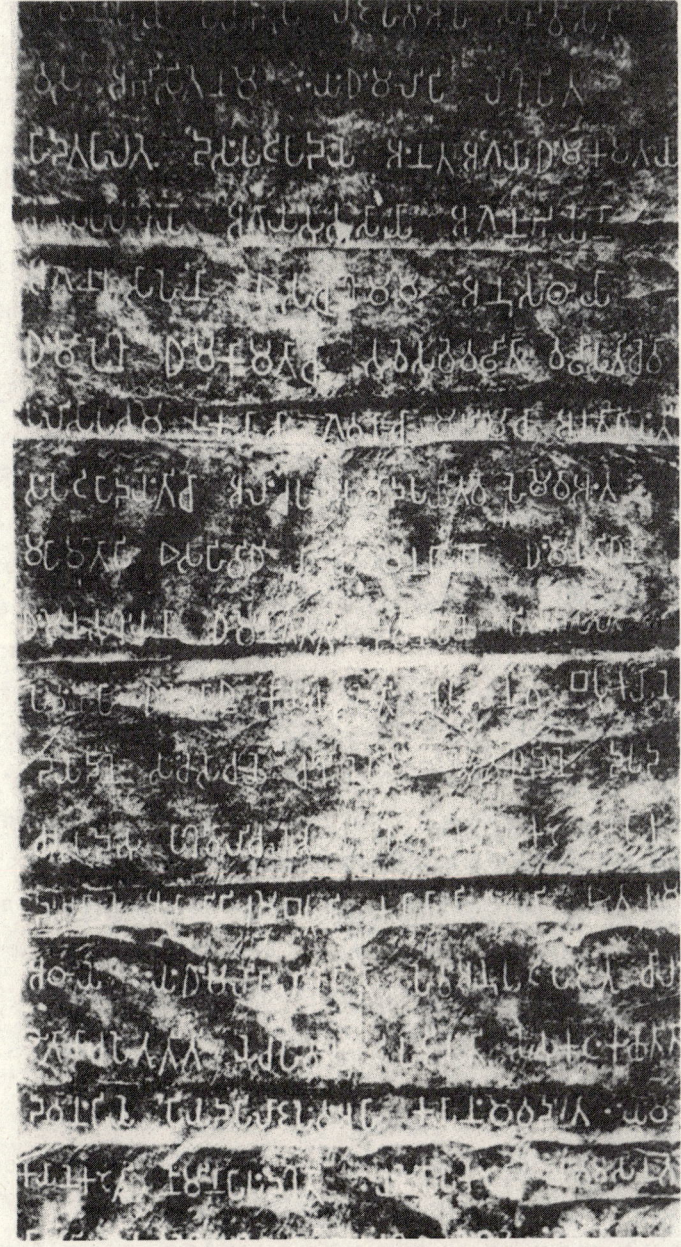

The Delhi-Topra pillar: north face
Courtesy: Archaeological Survey of India

at Firoz Shah Kotla. The pillars are tall shafts sculpted out of sandstone. The Delhi–Meerut pillar stands just over 32 feet high while the height of the Delhi–Topra pillar is 42 feet 7 inches. Judging from the capitals of Ashokan pillars found elsewhere, these two pillars were in all likelihood once surmounted by an inverted lotus supporting one or more animals sculpted in the round.

There is an important difference between the edict-bearing rocks and the two pillar edicts. The rock edict is *in situ*, i.e. in the original place where Ashoka had it inscribed, while the two pillars are not. Both were brought to Delhi, one from near Meerut (in Uttar Pradesh) and the other from Topra (near Ambala in Haryana) due to the enthusiasm of a medieval Sultan of Delhi, Firuz Shah Tughluq (1351–88 AD).

The sites selected for the inscribing of Ashoka's edicts were in some cases important places on the trade routes of the time, in others places that had some connection with the Buddha or Buddhism. Some sites combined both these features. The rock edict at Bahapur seems to be connected with the *Uttarapatha*—the great trans-regional trade route of north India. The northern artery of this route which swept across the Gangetic plains, linking the northwestern parts of the subcontinent to the Gangetic delta, passed through Delhi. It is an important fact that a Mughal *kos minar* (similar to modern mile-stones on highways) was located at Bahapur, confirming that in medieval times a major trade route passed this way. The fact that Ashoka's rock edict is found near this spot suggests that this was an important route in ancient times as well.

There is another possibility that would explain the location of the rock edicts at Bahapur Srinivaspuri. The rocks on which Ashoka's edict is inscribed lie at the base of a rocky stretch close to the temple of the goddess Kalka Devi (Kali). The present temple is a modern one, but is it possible (this is pure speculation!) that this place marks the site of an older shrine? If so, there may have been some additional point in Ashoka having his *dhamma* teachings with their emphasis on virtues such as *ahimsa* (non-injury) inscribed near a place where bloody sacrifices may have been performed to propitiate a firce and powerful goddess.[32]

Versions of Ashoka's Minor Rock Edict I have been found at several places in northern, central, and southern India.[33] In the Bahapur/Srinivaspuri version of the edict (which is shorter than the other versions), Ashoka tells us that he became a lay devotee of Buddhism (the word used is *upasaka*) two-and-a-half years ago, but that for a year he did not make much progress. After this, he had drawn closer to the Buddhist monastic order (*sangha*). Ashoka boasts that due to his efforts and exertions, gods and men had come to mingle in India (the word used for India is *Jambudvipa*). Ashoka points out that anybody, whether great and rich or humble and poor could follow *dhamma* and attain heaven. The edict tells us that this proclamation was being made so that the high and low, rich and poor, could exert themselves in following *dhamma* and in order that people living beyond the king's borders could also learn about this matter.

---

[32] Recently, an ugly concrete shelter has been built over the rock edict, an iron grill placed over the inscription for its protection, and the patch of land where the rocks lie enclosed by a stone wall. The fact of the matter is that this area serves both as a garbage dump and an open-air toilet for the villagers living nearby. This makes the experience of visiting the site not a very edifying one. A recent visit revealed the worst thing of all— that very little of the inscription survives beneath the iron grill.

[33] These occur at Ahraura in Uttar Pradesh; Sahasram in Bihar; Bairat in Rajasthan; Rupnath, Gujjara, and Panguraria in Madhya Pradesh; Erragudi and Rajula-Mandagiri in Andhra Pradesh; and Brahmagiri, Gavirmath, Maski, Palkigundu, Siddapura, Nittur, and Udegolam in Karnataka.

Translation of Ashoka's Edict at Bahapur

The Beloved of the Gods (Devanampiya)[34] says:

More than two-and-a-half years have passed since I became a Buddhist layman. But no great effort (in promoting the cause of *Dhamma*) was made by me. It is more than a year since I have drawn close to the Buddhist Order that I have exerted myself zealously. Those men who in the past did not mingle with the gods in Jambudvipa have come to mingle with them. This is the result of my exertions. And this (goal) is not one to be attained only by the great. Even a humble man who exerts himself (in cultivating *dhamma*) can attain heaven. This proclamation is made for the following purpose: Let the humble and the great exert themselves (in the pursuit of *dhamma*). And let even the people living beyond the borders of my kingdom know about this. And let exertion (in the cause of *dhamma*) endure forever. And this cause (of *dhamma*) will be furthered greatly among the people; it will increase one-and-a-half fold.

The Ashokan pillars generally carry six edicts, as in the case of the Delhi–Meerut pillar; however the Delhi–Topra pillar has seven. Their contents are related to the theme that Ashoka seems to have been obsessed with—*dhamma*.[35] The inscriptions describe

[31] This is one of the two epithets invariably used by Ashoka in his inscriptions; the other one is Piyadassi—'he who regards (others) amiably,' or alternatively 'of gracious appearance.' The name 'Ashoka' occurs only in a few versions of Minor Rock Edict (at Maski, Gujjara, Udegolam, and Nittur) and nowhere else.

[35] For the text and translation of the various Ashokan inscriptions, readers can consult *Corpus Inscriptionum Indicarum*, vol. 1, ed. by E. Hultzsch (1925). English translations of the inscriptions can also be found in D.C. Sircar's *Inscriptions of Asoka* (2nd revised edn., Delhi 1967) and Romila Thapar's *Asoka and the Decline of the Mauryas* (2nd edn., Delhi 1963). For the Prakrit text and an English translation of the Srinivaspuri/Bahapur rock edict, *see* M.C. Joshi and B.M. Pande, 'A newly-discovered inscription of Asoka at

dhamma as consisting of the following virtues: *ahimsa* (non-injury to all living beings), good deeds, mercy, charity, truthfulness, and purity. The king boasts of his exertions in spreading *dhamma* and expresses his satisfaction at the results. He talks of the duties of Mauryan officials known as the *rajukas* and *dhamma-mahamattas*— a special cadre of officials he created for the express purpose of spreading *dhamma*. He expresses his wish that there should be uniformity in judicial procedure all over his empire, and speaks of a three-day respite that he had granted to those who had been sentenced to death, and periodic releases of prisoners on humanitarian grounds. Ashoka also refers in the pillar edicts to his public welfare measures like planting trees, digging wells, and building rest-houses for the benefit of men and animals. He details the various species the killing of which he had banned in the twenty-seventh year after his consecration (*abhisheka*). Ashoka also talks of his respect for all religious sects. He admits in the seventh pillar edict that it is difficult to promote *dhamma* through legislation, and that persuasion is the most effective way to achieve this goal. He concludes by expressing the hope that his sons and great grandsons and all men would follow *dhamma* for as long as the sun and moon endure.

Few of Ashoka's subjects would have been able to read his pious prescriptions in stone, and the king reached out to a much larger audience by ensuring that his message was spread far and wide orally by an army of officials and by himself personally. This was the first massive state-supported propaganda campaign in Indian history.

Bahapur, Delhi,' *Journal of the Royal Asiatic Society of Great Britain and Ireland,* 1967, parts 3–4, pp. 96–8. *Also,* D.C. Sircar, 'New Delhi Inscription of Asoka,' *Epigraphia Indica,* 38 (1969–70), pp. 1–4.

The adventures of the Ashokan pillars in medieval and modern times
Ashoka would probably have been amazed (or more likely,
extremely annoyed) if he had known what would happen to two
of his edict-bearing pillars some fifteen centuries after his time.
We are very fortunate in having an account of how the two Ashokan
pillars were brought from Topra and Meerut to Delhi with great
care and effort and installed there during the time of Firuz Shah
Tughluq. Shams Siraj Afif tells in his chronicle the *Tarikh-i-Firuz
Shahi* of how the Sultan noticed the two columns in the course of
his military campaigns and had one (which came to be called the
Minar-i-Zarin or Golden Column) transported and erected in his
palace at Firuzabad near the banks of the Yamuna, and the other
in his Kushk-i-Shikar or Hunting Palace[36]

Afif writes that these two pillars dated from the time of the
Pandavas, and recounts a tradition that they had been the walking
sticks of the Pandava hero Bhima. We are told that the Sultan was
filled with admiration when he saw the pillars and decided to
move them to Delhi as trophies. The description of the moving of
the Delhi–Topra (Minar-i-Zarin) pillar tells of orders issued to
people living in and around Topra village, and also to soldiers,
directing them to assemble at the column, bringing with them
various implements and materials, including large quantities of
silk cotton from the *semal (S. malabarica)* tree. When the earth
around the column was carefully removed, it fell on the bed of
silk cotton that had been prepared for it. It was then encased in
reeds and raw hides and carefully moved onto a specially constructed carriage with forty-two wheels. Men pulled at the ropes attached
to the wheels, and in this manner the pillar slowly made its way to
the banks of the Yamuna. Here the Sultan came in person to meet

[36] H.M. Elliot and J. Dowson, *The History of India as Told by Its Own Historians: Tarikh-i
Firoz Shahi of Shams-i Siraj Afif*(Calcutta, 1953 reprint), pp. 91–5.

it. The pillar was then heaved onto several boats tied together and taken by river to its new home in Delhi. At Firuzabad, it was raised to its present postion in the palace complex with great ingenuity, skill, and labour.

The writing on the Ashokan pillars could no longer be read by Firuz Shah's time. Afif tells us that some Brahmins gave the interpretation that the inscription on one of them contained a prophecy that no one would be able to remove the pillar from its place till the time of a great king named Sultan Firuz. The reading was too contrived to convince anyone, even a king who might have found it flattering. Afif tells us that some years later, when the Mongol Timur invaded India, he visited the monuments of former kings and was very impressed by these remarkable pillars.

Yet another aspect of the medieval history of the two Ashokan pillars is inscribed on their surface. Below the Ashokan edicts, the Delhi–Meerut pillar bears three short early fourteenth century Sanskrit inscriptions. The first refers to a person named Virapala, son of a ruler of Sind. The second, also of the fourteenth century, refers to the writer as a gold-smith named Mala Saha. The third inscription belongs to the sixteenth century. It says that it was written by a person named Amara and contains certain words, the meaning of which is unclear. Who the people mentioned in these three inscriptions were and what they intended to convey through these inscriptions which they had inscribed on the Ashokan pillar, we do not know.

The Delhi–Topra pillar bears three twelfth century inscriptions of the Chauhan Rajput king Visaladeva alias Vigraharajaraja (IV).[37] In one of them, the king boasts of his conquests from the Himalayas to the Vindhyas and of his exterminating the *mlechchhas* (outsiders

---

[37] For more on Vigraharaja IV, see chapter 8.

or barbarians, referring in this case to the Turks) and restoring Aryavarta—the land of the Aryas—to what its name signified. The pillar also bears two sixteenth-century epigraphs. The first is a short Sanskrit inscription giving the date and the name of the writer, a person named Ama. The second, longer inscription in mixed Sanskrit and Persian refers to Sultan Ibrahim and states that the inscription was written by Viyada, son of Sayana. There is also a reference to a person named Bahadur Khan. Sultan Ibrahim may be identified with the sixteenth century Lodi king of that name, while Bahadur Khan may have been a nobleman during his reign.

The medieval accounts of the moving of the Ashokan pillars to Delhi and the medieval inscriptions they bear introduce us to an important aspect of certain historical monuments—the changes and redefinition of what they mean and what they stand for. They show us how a monument of one age can be given an entirely new meaning in another. We can see this sort of thing around us even today, for instance in the conversion of medieval palaces into hotels. In this particular case, Firuz Shah Tughluq was impressed by two monolithic pillars made and erected over a thousand years before his time by a Mauryan emperor. He did not know what the original purpose of the pillars may have been; neither did he have any idea of what the writing on the pillar said. He brought the columns to Delhi and had them set up in two prominent places. When the pillars were fixed in their new locales, Afif tells us that certain additions were made to them—ornamental friezes of black and white stone were added to the top, and a guilded cupola was placed on the pinnacle. Changes in the physical appearance of the Asokan pillars were accompanied by continuity and change in the meaning of the monuments. The pillars had been imperial monuments, symbols of a king's power and dominion in Ashoka's time. Firuz Shah Tughluq relocated them and took them over as monuments signifying his *own* power and dominion. But, in their newer medieval setting, the edict-bearing pillars were no longer conveyors of the *dhamma* message of the earlier king.

The adventures of the Delhi–Meerut pillar did not end with its journey from Meerut to Delhi. Writing in the 1860s, the great archaeologist Sir Alexander Cunningham describes it as lying in five pieces near Hindu Rao's house on the top of the hill.[38] He writes that according to popular belief, the pillar had broken into pieces due to the accidental explosion of a magazine of gun-powder during the time of the late Mughal king Farukhsiyar. The combined length of the five pieces was 32 ¾ ft., but the upper section of the middle piece which bore Ashoka's edicts had been sawn off some years earlier and sent off to the Asiatic Society's museum in Calcutta. This piece was ultimately brought back to Delhi and the fragments of the pillar joined together. Cunningham notes in his reports that in his opinion, the reconstituted pillar should have been set up at Meerut, where it originally stood

The story of ancient monuments includes the rediscovery of their historical significance in modern times. European travelers and visitors who saw the two Ashokan pillars in Delhi have left us with their impressions of what they saw. Referring to the Delhi–Topra pillar, the nineteenth-century European traveler Tom Coryat narrated in a letter to one L. Whittaker that in 'Delee' he saw a

---

[38] It seems rather inappropriate to relegate Sir Alexander Cunningham to a foot-note; the sole motive in doing so is not to break the flow of the main narrative. Cunningham (1814–93)—soldier, military surveyor and engineer, archaeologist, scholar—was a towering figure in Indian archaeology in the second half of the nineteenth century. He became the first Director-General of the Archaeological Survey of India in 1871. Using the accounts of the Chinese pilgrims Hsuan-tsang and Fa-hsien as a guide, Cunningham surveyed and documented details of hundreds of sites in north India in the course of a series of field surveys the sweep of which was unprecedented and remains unmatched till today. Cunningham's reports make fascinating and exciting reading and remain an important source of information on a variety of subjects, including the history of Delhi.

brazen pillar erected by the Macedonian king Alexander to mark his victory over his arch Indian adversary Porus.[39] Coryat passed on similar incorrect information to Chaplain Edward Terry who wrote in his journal that Coryat had told him that he had seen a pillar of *marble* with a Greek inscription. Coryat probably jumped to the conclusion that the pillar bore a Greek inscription because of the similarity between certain Greek and Brahmi letters. However, his claims about the contents of the inscription were obviously quite fanciful. It is also interesting to note that he thought that the pillar was made of either brass or marble. Another contemporary traveller, Bishop Heber, described the pillar as 'a high black pillar of cast metal' and likened it to the iron pillar in the Qutb complex. Such mistakes about the material of which the Delhi–Topra pillar was made may have been in part due to its unusual, lustrous surface.

The redefinition of the meaning of historical remains of the past is an ongoing process. We can end this account of the Ashokan pillars by taking note of the fact that there are places where Ashokan pillars or fragments of such pillars are today being worshipped as Shiva *lingas*. What an amazing transformation of meaning!

[39] The adventurous and eccentric Thomas Coryat was a man who devoted his life to travelling and writing about his travels. He called himself 'the Odeombian Gallo-Belgic leg-stretcher,' alluding to his birth-place and his extensive travels on foot. His book on his continental walking tour through parts of France, Italy, Switzerland, and Germany was entitled *Coryat's Crudities, hastily gobled in five months travells*. Walking across Asia, he turned up in the court of the Mughal emperor Jahangir, and appears to have given a speech in Persian to the emperor in which he gave four reasons for his coming to India: to see the great Mughal emperor, the emperor's elephants and the Ganga, and to get the emperor's permission to visit Timur's tomb in Samarkand. Coryat lost many of his notes on his Asiatic journeys. One set was published during his life time, while extracts from the others appeared in print posthumously. Coryat died in Surat in December, 1617. He lies buried somewhere on the banks of the Tapti river.

6

Between Two Empires

The Mauryan empire came to an end in about 181/180 BC when the last Mauryan emperor Brihadratha was assassinated while reviewing his troops by his commander-in-chief, Pushyamitra Shunga. Pushyamitra was the first ruler of the Shunga dynasty (181–75 BC). His empire extended up to the Narbada and included Pataliputra, Ayodhya, and Vidisha; in the northwest, it may have included Jalandhara and Sakala. The Delhi region fell within the Shunga domain. An invasion of the Bactrian Greeks (probably under Demetrios) was repulsed, and Pushyamitra is credited with having performed the *ashvamedha* sacrifice on two occasions. In the Magadha region in the east, the Shungas were succeeded by the Kanva and then the Mitra kings.

The second century BC to the second century AD was a period when tribal movements in Central Asia came to have their reverberations in the Indian subcontinent, taking the form of a series of invasions from the north-west. In earlier centuries, inroads made by the Persians under Cyrus and Darius, and the invasion of Alexander of Macedon (326 BC) had scarcely touched the fringes of the subcontinent. Now, Greeks from Bactria (the Balkh region to the south of the Oxus river), Shakas or Scythians (from the plains of the Syr Darya), Pahlavas or Parthians (originally from Iran), and the Kushanas (a branch of the Yueh Chi tribe of Central Asia) entered India and carved out empires. Some of these, such as the empire of the Indo-Greeks or Indo-Bactrians, were comparatively short-lived, while others such as that of the Shakas had a longer lease of life. Indo-Greek and the Parthian rule seem to have been confined to the north-western part of the Indian subcontinent, but the Shakas and Kushanas moved further afield. The Shakas settled in central and western India, and kings of Shaka stock continued to rule in some of these parts till the second or third centuries AD. Another large empire was the Kushana empire, which at its zenith included portions of modern Uttar Pradesh and the Punjab in India, and the North West Frontier Province and Bahawalpur regions of Pakistan.

The influx of people belonging to a large variety of ethnic groups had more than a political significance. It led to a series of interactions which had a cultural dimension as well. A classic example of this is the Gandhara school of art, which displayed the coming together of Indian (particularly Buddhist) themes and Graeco-Roman style.

The collapse of the Kushana empire in the middle of the third century AD made way for the resurgence of several monarchical and non-monarchical states in north India. The so-called 'tribal republics' included the Arjunayanas (who were initially settled in the Bharatpur and Alwar area), the Malavas (who moved from the Punjab into the Rajasthan area), and the Yaudheyas (who established themselves in eastern Punjab and the adjoining areas of Uttar Pradesh and Rajasthan). We know about these people mainly from their coins, seals, and inscriptions. It is possible that the Arjunayanas and Yaudheyas exercised some control over the Delhi area. It is interesting that the names of both these peoples can be connected with the *Mahabharata* legend—the Arjunayanas perhaps claiming descent from the epic hero Arjuna, the Yaudheyas (from '*yodha*,' warrior) from his elder brother Yudhishthira.

Situated as it was in the corridor between the Indus basin and the Ganga valley, Delhi directly experienced many of the political vicissitudes of this period, but these have not left a very clear mark. The only direct evidence of any of the invasions mentioned above comes from stray coins of some of these dynasties. In fact, the testimony of archaeology presents something of a contrast to the turbulent political history of the period. It suggests continuity of occupation at many sites and reveals the details of the rather placid every-day life of people. Literary as well as archaeological evidence from various parts of the subcontinent gives us a picture of expanding urban centres and flourishing trade.

There is an interesting reference in a text belonging to this period which may be relevant for our story of Delhi's past. The text is Ptolemy's *Treatise on Geography* (a sequel to the *Almagest*, his famous work on astronomy). Ptolemy was an exceptionally versatile second century AD Alexandrian scholar, famed as a mathematician, musician, astronomer, and geographer. In his *Treatise on Geography,* he listed various places in India, giving their latitude and longitude. Daiddala and Indapat occur in his list. Cunningham suggested the possibility that Ptolemy's Daiddala may be identified with Delhi and Indapat with Indraprastha. The latitude and longitude given by Ptolemy do not in fact match exactly with these places, but even if we make some allowances, at least one of the identifications suggested by Cunningham can be questioned. While Ptolemy's Indapat may well be identified with Indraprastha, which is a very ancient place name, it is difficult to identify Daiddala with Delhi. The most important objection is that the earliest clear references to a settlement in the Delhi area going by the name of

Dilli (or one of the several variants of the name) belong to the early medieval period, and post-date Ptolemy by several centuries.

Evidence from the Purana Qila and other sites

At the Purana Qila in Delhi, we have more details about the second century BC to the second/third century AD levels than for the preceding phases. In the early part of this period, houses were built of quartzite rubble set in mud mortar; later houses were made of mud brick and burnt bricks. House floors were usually made of rammed earth and sometimes paved with mud bricks. Among the miscellaneous items found were a small anthropomorphic pot, and several terracotta plaques depicting *yakshas* (popular deities associated with fertility and prosperity), *yakshis* (the female counterparts of *yakshas*), goddesses, couples, a female lute player, and elephant-riders. Animal and human figurines including one depicting a human head with an ornate cap, beads, and bone points were also unearthed. A seal and several sealings[40] bore the names of various individuals (e.g. Patithaka, Svatiguta, Usasena, Thiya) in the Brahmi script. Sherds of stamped pottery, skin rubbers, fragments of a votive tank,[41] a small piece of an ivory handle, crucibles, and a few copper coins of the Kushanas and the Yaudheyas were among the reported finds. We can note the richness in quantity, quality, and range of the terracottas of this period compared to the earlier phase.

The site of Mandoli also has levels (Periods IV A and IV B) belonging to this period. Period IV A yielded a red pottery, some hand-made and some made on the wheel. The pottery was of medium to coarse fabric and bore stamped and incised designs. There were carinated *handis* (cooking pots), spouted vessels, spouts

[40] A sealing is a piece of clay on which the seal is impressed.
[41] These are hand-modeled miniature tanks which had some religious/ritualistic significance.

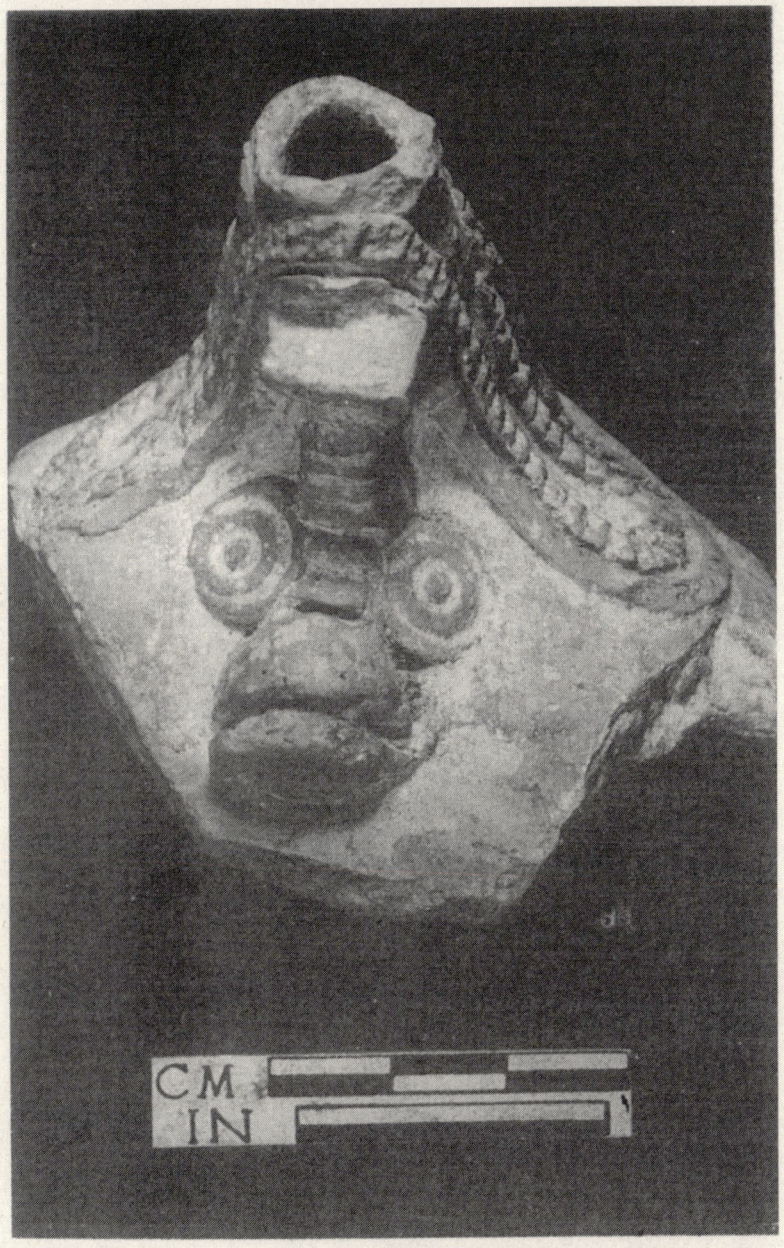

Purana Qila: anthropomorphic pot
Courtesy: Archaeological Survey of India

Purana Qila: terracotta plaque
Courtesy: Archaeological Survey of India

Purana Qila: terracotta head
Courtesy: Archaeological Survey of India

Purana Qila: incised and stamped pottery
Courtesy: Archaeological Survey of India

and miniature vessels. Terracotta animal figurines, gamesmen (small terracotta pieces which may have been used as counters in some sort of ancient version of a board-game), objects made of shell, earrings, and fishing net weights were also found. In one of the trenches, archaeologists found the remains of a house complex made of mud. In the later part of this period (IV B), the houses were better built and made of burnt bricks. Two successively built floors of mud and lime and a hearth were found in one of the rooms of a house. Human and animal figurines made of terracotta, beads of semi-precious stone, shell objects, a terracotta plumb-bob (a spherical object which, suspended from a string, is used to determine the perpendicularity of walls), dabbers (clay spatulas pressed against the interior of pots to maintain their form while they are being beaten into shape), copper rings, and iron objects such as arrow-heads, sickles, and spear-heads were discovered. Copper coins belonging to the reign of the Kushana king Vasudeva (II) and the rim of a vase bearing Brahmi letters typical of the Kushana period are among the other significant finds of this period.

Mandoli: inscribed rim fragment
Courtesy: Department of Archaeology, Government of India

The report on the Mandoli excavations suggests that the settlement had grown into a prosperous town during the first two centuries of the Christian era.

At Bhorgarh, the levels belonging to the early centuries AD can be divided into two phases. In the earlier phase, houses were made of mud bricks; in the second there was a transition to the use of burnt bricks. A hearth was found in one of the structures. Terracotta beads and figurines of humans and animals, two terracotta sealings bearing an inscription in the Brahmi script (reading 'Supakasa'), implements of various kinds (the report does not specify their nature), and copper coins were also found.

Apart from the evidence from these excavated sites, pottery (including the typical red ware of this period) and sculptural fragments belonging roughly to the second century BC to the fourth century AD have been found in many other places in and around Delhi. To the east of Nachauli village, a red sandstone *linga* (which

Tilpat: cross-bar with lotus medallion

Photograph: N. Lahiri

seems to belong stylistically to the early centuries AD) lies in the middle of the fields. In the southern and northern part of the village of Tilpat of *Mahabharata* fame, large sized bricks of the Kushana or the Gupta period have been found. A more striking find were four red sandstone *suchis* (cross-bars) with carved lotus medallions in the courtyard of a village resident. These suggest that there may have been a Buddhist or Jaina complex near Tilpat during the early centuries of the Christian era.

It is interesting to note the fact that in certain instances, villagers have collected old sculptural fragments discovered over the years in their village and assembled them in shrines. Such shrines (*grama-sthana*) are associated with the village and village community as a whole, and worshippers who come here have varied religious, class, and caste backgrounds. What we have here is not a simple case of old religious images being worshipped in modern times. Not all the sculptural fragments that are placed in these often open-air shrines seem originally to have been *murtis* or religious icons. The images are frequently so damaged that it is difficult to ascertain *what* they once represented. The intriguing thing is that what they originally represented seems to bear little relevance to how they are understood by the people who come to pray and place offerings at these shrines. There are cases, for instance, where old *murtis* of male gods such as Ganesha and Vishnu are being worshipped as part of mother goddess (*mata*) shrines. And again, where there are a number of sculptural pieces, sanctity seems to be attributed to them as a group rather than to them individually. This phenomenon, which forms a part of the religious life of many village communities, finds no mention whatsoever in the great Sanskrit texts. In fact, the scriptural tradition strictly forbids the worship of broken or mutilated images. It just goes to show that there is a big difference between textual religion and religious practice, between what the books say and what people do.

What we have before us is a fascinating example of how remains of the ancient and early medieval past have been integrated into modern-day religious life, and have acquired in the process a new meaning and significance. Once these sculptural fragments are placed in the village shrine, they become part of the common cultural heritage of the village. What has happened in this process is that villagers have, in a natural and unselfconscious way, become the custodians of the heritage of their village. Past and present blend in the rural landscape in the most casual and yet remarkable manner.

7

The Legend of the Iron Column

In the fourth and fifth centuries AD, kings such as Chandragupta I (319–35/36 AD), Samudragupta (335–70 AD), and Chandragupta II (375–413/14 AD) launched a series of successful military campaigns and established their political domination over a large part of the Indian subcontinent. The Gupta kings proclaimed their political power and imperial status *vis-a-vis* other, lesser, kings of their time through the use of grand titles such as *maharajadhiraja* (great king of kings), *parama-bhattaraka* (one supremely entitled to reverence) and *parameshvara* (great lord), setting new fashions in royal rhetoric.

The Gupta period is considered a 'golden age' by some historians because it was an age which saw the (re-)emergence of a large empire, and a remarkable level of cultural achievement. The term 'classical age' is also sometimes used to highlight the fact that in many spheres of art and literature, the Gupta period represents a high water-mark, setting for later ages standards that were emulated but never surpassed. Other historians have questioned the need of identifying the Gupta (or any other period in Indian history for that matter) as a 'golden age.' While acknowledging the cultural achievements of this period, it has been suggested that the Gupta empire was not a cohesive structure but a loosely-knit decentralized empire, and that this period saw political, economic, and social developments that add up to what can be described as an Indian brand of feudalism. A decline in trade, urban centres, and coinage are other features of this alternative portrayal of the Gupta age.

During the reigns of the later Gupta kings, the empire gradually declined, partly due to internal problems and weakening, in part due to competition from contemporary dynasties such as the Vakatakas who ruled over the western Deccan. Then, in the fifth century, a new political factor made its appearance as a branch of the Hunas gradually fanned out from their base in the Oxus valley towards Iran and India. Crossing the Hindu Kush mountains, they occupied Gandhara and from there, surged into the interior of India. One of their invasions was successfully repulsed by the Gupta king Skandagupta. But the progress of the Hunas was inexorable and later Gupta kings were not able to keep them at bay. Under their chiefs Toramana and his successor Mihirakula, the Hunas moved into Kashmir and the Punjab and thence into parts of Uttar Pradesh, Rajasthan, and western India. They became a spent force some time in the sixth century AD.

The iron pillar at Mehrauli

The most striking monument of the Gupta period in Delhi is the inscribed iron pillar situated in the courtyard of the Jami Masjid (today known as the Quwwat-ul-Islam mosque) in the Qutb complex. Once again, we see the ancient and medieval past rubbing shoulders. The inscription is inscribed on the west face of a 23 ft. 8 inches high iron column which tapers slightly from a diameter of sixteen inches at the base to twelve inches at the top. The column is surmounted by a capital in the form of an inverted lotus (3' 6" high). A motif imbued with rich meaning in several ancient cultures, the lotus is a symbol of purity and fecundity. The pillar was probably originally crowned by a Vaishnava emblem, perhaps a *garuda* (the mythical eagle, the vehicle of the god Vishnu). The language of the six-line inscription is Sanskrit, the script Brahmi.

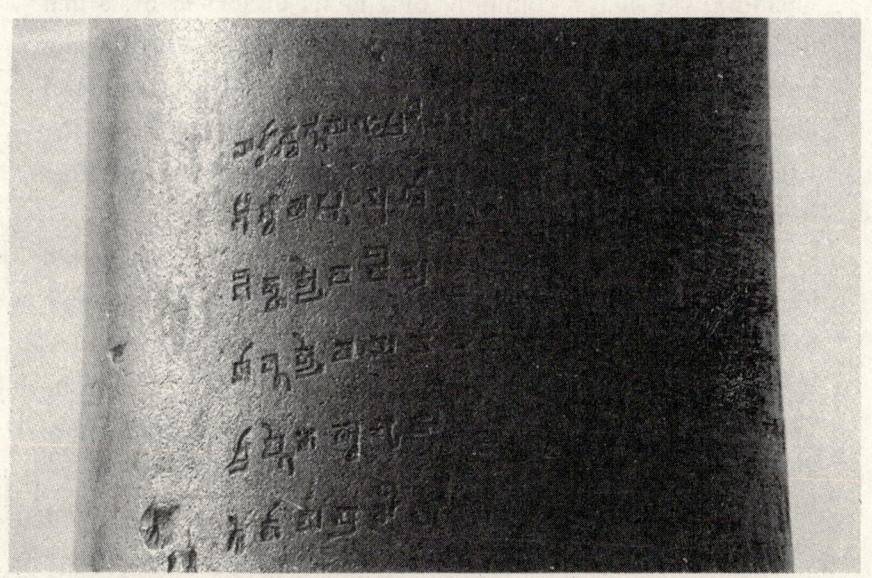

The inscription of king Chandra
Photograph: Aditya Arya

James Prinsep, the scholar who deciphered the Brahmi letters of the Ashokan inscriptions, also tried his hand at reading the inscription on the iron pillar. The script of the Mehrauli iron pillar inscription is a later form of the Brahmi of Ashokan times. Prinsep thought that the inscription referred to a king named Dhava, and although he was later proved to be wrong on this point, he got a lot of other things right—the general tenor of the contents of the inscription as also its age, which on palaeographic grounds, he placed in the third or fourth century AD.[42] Cunningham preferred to read the name of the king in question as Bhava. He suggested that Bhava might have been a king who played a part in the downfall of the Gupta dynasty.

The king whose exploits the Mehrauli iron pillar speaks of was not in fact Dhava or Bhava but Chandra. The problem was that Chandra was such a common royal name in ancient India that historians were not sure *which* of the various Chandras the inscription was talking about (the inscription bears no date and gives no genealogy). Today, there is general agreement that the Chandra of the Mehrauli iron pillar inscription should be identified with the Gupta emperor Chandragupta II (375–413 AD).

The inscription describes a king named Chandra 'on whose arm fame was inscribed by the sword.' This king had a countenance as beauteous as the full moon (there is a pun on the word 'chandra' here). The inscription speaks of his beating back in battle the enemies from Vanga (Bengal) who united to advance against him, and his victory over the Vahlikas (who seem to have lived in the Punjab region) after crossing the Sindhu (Indus) river. Having fixed his mind with devotion on the god Vishnu, king Chandra set up this flag-staff of Vishnu on the Vishnupada hill.[43] Evoking powerful imagery, the inscription tells us that although the king was no more, his fame remained on the earth like the smouldering embers of a great forest fire that has died out. It seems likely that while the pillar was erected during the life-time of king Chandra,

---

[42] Palaeography is the study of the evolution of old scripts.
[43] For the Sanskrit text (and English translation) of the inscription, *see* John Faithul Fleet, *Corpus Inscriptionum Indicarum*, vol. 3, pp. 258-9.

the inscription was inscribed some time after his death.[44] This would account for its somewhat melancholy tone.

Translation of the Mehrauli iron pillar inscription of Chandra

(Verse 1) On whose arm fame was inscribed by the sword, when in battle in the Vanga country, he repulsed with his breast the enemies who, joining together, had advanced against him; by whom, crossing the seven mouths of the Sindhu, the Vahlikas were conquered in battle; by the breeze of whose valour the southern ocean is still perfumed ...

(Verse 2) He, the lord of men, whose body, as though weary, has departed from this earth to another world (heaven) won by his deeds, but who remains on this earth in his fame; whose great glory, the result of his destruction of his enemies, does not yet leave this earth like the heat (from the smouldering embers) of a now quiet fire in a great forest ...

(Verse3) By that king, who acquired supreme sovereignty on earth for a very long time by his own prowess (and) who, having the name Chandra and a beauty of countenance resembling the full-moon, having fixed his mind with devotion on Vishnu, this lofty standard of the lord Vishnu was set up on the Vishnupada hill.

We do not know for sure where the iron pillar originally stood. Most historians believe that the iron pillar is not *in situ*. This is

[44] While the inscription is considered a posthumous one by most scholars, there are some, such as D.R. Bhandarkar, who think otherwise. See the edition of *Corpus Inscriptionum Indicarum*, vol. 3, revised by D.R. Bhandarkar and edited by B. Chhabra and G.S. Gai (New Delhi, 1981, p. 57).

because the inscription refers to the pillar being installed on a hill named Vishnupada and there is nothing quite resembling a hill at the present site.[45] On the other hand, the renowned epigraphist J.F. Fleet pointed out that the underground supports of the column include several small pieces of metal which seem to have been part of its original underpinnings, not the sorts of things that would have been brought along if the pillar had indeed been transported here from somewhere else. The counter-argument to this is the example of the Delhi–Topra pillar of Ashoka that was brought to Delhi from Topra, foundation stone and all. The possibility that the original location of the Mehrauli pillar was in or around Delhi, perhaps near or even *at* the present site cannot be ruled out, especially in view of the sculptural remains indicative of a large temple complex that have been unearthed in the excavations at Lal Kot nearby. We may note that the legend that connects Anangapala Tomara with the pillar talks of his digging up and then replanting the pillar, not moving it to some other location.[46]

Just as in the case of the Delhi–Topra pillar of the Mauryan period, there is confusion in early modern notices about the material out of which the Mehrauli pillar was made. These notices are cited by Alexander Cunningham in his archaeological reports for the years 1862–3 and 1864–5. In 1805, the pillar was described by a European woman tourist in a tract entitled *Tour in the Upper Provinces* as 'the wonderful brazen pillar.' Bishop Heber described it as a 'black pillar of cast metal.' A Miss Emma Roberts (in a tract entitled *Views in India*) referred to it as 'a pillar of mixed metal.' Major-General Sir W.H. Sleeman (famed for his efforts to eradicate 'thuggee') refers to it in his *Rambles and Recollections of an Indian*

---

[15] According to D.R. Bhandarkar (*op. cit.*), Vishnupada was located in the Himalayas, close to the source of the Beas river.

[16] Details of this legend are given later in this chapter.

Official as a small pillar of bronze or a metal that resembles bronze. Cunningham himself initially thought that the pillar was made of some sort of 'mixed metal' similar to bronze. However, an analysis he had made of a small piece from the lower part of the pillar showed it to be made of pure malleable iron of 7.66 specific gravity. Cunningham suggested that the idea that the pillar was made of bronze perhaps arose because of the yellowish appearance of the upper part of the shaft.

The most remarkable aspect of the Mehrauli iron pillar is that it has remained rust-free for so many centuries. Modern analysis has shown that it is made of very pure wrought iron with a high phosphorus and a low carbon, sulphur and manganese content. The composition does not, however, fully explain how the pillar has evaded rust for so many centuries.

The iron pillar also bears several other short inscriptions. There is an eleventh-century inscription which seems to refer to the Tomara king Anangapala establishing Delhi. An early eighteenth-century inscription refers to the Bundela kings of Chanderi. Two nineteenth-century inscriptions refer to a person named Raja Chhatra Sinha who claimed to be a descendent of the Chauhan king Rai Pithora. Two seventeenth-century Persian inscriptions give the names of certain individuals who may have visited the place.

The iron pillar in medieval legend

At some point of time, we don't know exactly when, the Gupta iron pillar got tied up in local legend and folk-lore with the Rajput king Anangapala of the Tomara clan and with a story of how the city of Delhi got its name. Writing in the nineteenth century, Cunningham recorded what he described as a 'universal tradition' current in his time that the iron pillar had been erected by the

Rajput king Bilan Deo or Anangapala Tomara. A version of the
legend is contained in Book III of the Rajasthani epic, the *Prithviraja
Raso*, in an episode entitled *Killi-dhilli-katha*. The broad outline
of the legend is as follows: A learned Brahmin told king Anangapala
that the base of the pillar had been driven so deep into the ground
that it rested on the hood of Vasuki, the king of serpents who
supports the world from below. The pillar was immovable, and as
long as the pillar stood, prophesied the Brahmin, so long would
Anangapala's dominion last. Now, instead of being sensible and
accepting this prophecy and leaving the pillar alone, Anangapala
decided to check things out for himself. He ordered the pillar dug
up. When the lowermost portion emerged from beneath the
ground, it was covered with the blood of the serpent king Vasuki,
whose head it had pierced. The king, realizing that he had made
a terrible mistake, immediately ordered the pillar to be reinstalled.
But every effort to fix the pillar firmly in the ground failed. The
pillar remained loose (*dhili*) and, so the story concludes, in the
looseness and shakiness of the pillar lies the origin of the name of
the city of Delhi.

In another version of the legend, the prophecy is made not by
some ordinary Brahmin but by the great sage Vyasa and it is a
long nail or spike that pierces Vasuki's head. When restored, only
nineteen fingers' length of the pillar goes into the ground. The
sage tells the king that his dynasty would be unstable (*dhilli*) like
the spike (*killi*) he had driven in, and that after nineteen generations,
it would be supplanted by the Chauhans and then the Turks.[47]

There is a tradition that when Qutb-ud-din Aibak took over
Delhi, he was told by helpful informants that Hindu rule would
last as long as the iron pillar remained standing. We are told that

---

[47] These legends have been documented by Sir Alexander Cunningham in vol. 1 of his
    reports (those of the years 1862–5).

the conqueror displayed his confidence in himself and contempt for the prophecy by allowing the pillar to stand. The Jami Masjid was built close to the pillar, and the courtyard of that mosque encloses it.

The history of the iron pillar of Chandra thus spans many ages as it came to be entwined with pan-Indian and local legends of the early medieval period. In modern times, the pillar has come to be connected with a different kind of belief—that the person who stands with her back against it and manages to make the fingers of the two hands meet will have her wish come true. How serious this belief is, is of course a matter of conjecture. It is the kind of story that local tourist guides might have invented in order to liven things up for tourists. Regardless of its origins, it forms part of the modern folklore about Chandra's iron pillar. [48]

Remains of the Gupta period at the Purana Qila and elsewhere
From the exploits of kings and the legends that have grown around them, we turn to the more mundane details of the life of people living in Delhi and its neighbourhood roughly between the fourth and the sixth centuries AD. At the Purana Qila, levels belonging to the Gupta period revealed the remains of structures made of reused baked bricks of the earlier period. The notable finds included moulded pottery, including a lid bearing the motif of a *kinnara* (a creature half man, half horse), and a damaged terracotta female figurine. A terracotta seal bore the outline of a conch above and the legend 'Gopasya' (of or belonging to Gopa) below. Another seal read 'jitam bhagavata,' (victory to the *bhagavata*, i.e. the god Vasudeva Krishna), while a third bore the legend 'Sri traividya' in

---

[48] A recent visit to the Qutb revealed that the Archaeological Survey has erected an iron railing aroung the pillar. This has put a forcible end to the popular practice referred to here.

Brahmi letters of the Gupta period. The 1970–1 excavations
unearthed a building of this period which had gone through three
or four stages of construction. Initially, the structure was oblong in
plan with a partition wall. Then, a verandah or a room with a
rounded corner was added in front. Still later, the floor levels
were raised, steps added, and two partition walls were constructed
inside. A 60 cm. high brick pedestal with a stepped base was built
against one of the walls beside the entrance. In the last phase,
another verandah was built in front, the floor levels were raised
even further, and more steps added. A sealing inscribed with
Brahmi letters of the Gupta period and a gold-plated coin of the
archer type with the legend 'Shri Vikrama' were found embedded
in the debris of the last structural phase. Other antiquities found at
Gupta-period levels included a few human figurines made of
terracotta, a piece of carved shell bangle, a small damaged
sandstone *mukha-linga*, and painted pots. There were also sealings
with the legends 'Shri Makarasya' and 'Shri Aryyavama (?),' with
what seems to be a fire altar above the writing, and another sealing
with the legend 'Shri Gudhadasah' and a set of foot-prints below.
The people whose names occur on the sealings may have been
traders or officials, but we do not know this for sure.

The site of Mandoli also has occupational levels of the Gupta
period. Here, fragments of red polished ware of various shapes
were found. A terracotta sealing decorated with a conch at the top
and bearing an inscription in Brahmi characters of the Gupta period
was also discovered.

Isolated remains of pottery and sculpture found in various
villages in and around Delhi bear further testimony to the period.
As mentioned in an earlier chapter, such sculptural fragments often
form a part of village shrines. One of the most beautiful pieces of
sculpture which can on stylistic grounds be assigned to the Gupta

period is a black stone *mukhalinga* at Gothra Mohabbatabad, a village in the Faridabad district (located in the hills a few km. west of Pali). The *linga* is almost entirely covered with the carving of the face of Shiva, his eyes closed in an expression of serene meditation. The sculpture lies embedded in a whitewashed

Gothra Mohabbatabad *mukhalinga*
Photograph: N. Lahiri

concrete platform within a temple complex, just outside the cave
in which, according to local tradition, the ancient seer Uddalaka
performed his *tapasya*.

The post-Gupta phase

The decline of the Gupta empire in the late-fifth and early-sixth-
centuries was accompanied by the rise of various other dynasties
which ruled in different parts of north India. The Hunas became
a spent force, and gradually came to be assimilated into Indian
society; they were eventually accepted as one of the thirty-six Rajput
clans. The Maukharis carved out a kingdom in northern and eastern
India with their capital at Kanyakubja. To their west were the
Pushyabhutis of Sthanishvar (modern Thaneswar in Ambala
district). The Maukharis and Pushyabhutis were linked by a
matrimonial alliance. The most famous Pushyabhuti king was
Harshavardhana. Harshavardhana forms the subject of the
Harshacharita, a biography composed by his court poet Bana
Bhatta, and is also spoken of in the travel account of the Chinese
pilgrim, Hsuan-tsang.

Harshavardhana's empire seems to have included eastern
Punjab, parts of Uttar Pradesh, and also territories lying further
east. In Kanauj, the Pushyabhutis eventually made way in the early-
eighth-century for Yashovarman, a king immortalized in a Prakrit
work called the *Gaudavaho* (literally, 'the slaying of the king of
Gauda') written by his court poet Vakpati. Then, in the ninth
century, the Pratihara Rajputs established themselves as a major
political power in northern India, ruling from Kanauj. It is difficult
to get a clear idea of the contours of the empires of these and
other early medieval Indian kings. The enthusiastic accounts of
court poets give a larger-than-life portrayal of the personalities and
achievements of their patrons. The evidence suggests that the Delhi

region came consecutively under the rule of the Pushyabhutis, Yashovarman, and then the Pratiharas.

While we have a mass of detail about the various dynasties within whose domain the Delhi area came to be included, we know very little about the lives of ordinary people who lived here during the sixth to eighth centuries. Some structures of the post-Gupta period were revealed during the Purana Qila excavations. Several ovens, some resembling modern tandoors were found. Sherds of various types of red pottery, fragments of terracotta figurines, beads, and a damaged stone sculpture were among the other finds. Reused bricks (mud bricks as well as burnt bricks) and sagging walls tell their story of this phase.

8

The Time of the Rajputs

The early medieval period saw the rise of a number of new ruling clans in north India, described collectively in later histories as the Rajputs. The Rajput clans were of diverse origins and their rise to power can be connected with the expansion of agrarian settlement and state formation to hitherto peripheral areas. Two of these clans—the Tomaras and the Chauhans or Chahamanas—are closely associated with Delhi's history.

The seventeenth century Persian chronicler Muhammad Kasim Ferishta recounts a legend current in his time about the founding of Delhi: There was a pious, brave, and generous king named Dilu or Dhilu. He built the city of Delhi, which came to be named after him. In the fortieth year of his reign, Dilu was taken prisoner and confined in the fortress of Rhotas by Phur, a prince of his own family and governor of Kumaon. Phur is further described as an adversary of Alexander's and going by the name can perhaps be identified with Porus. Various versions of the legend of king Dilu are found in other medieval accounts. However, these, along with the tradition that Dilli was founded by king Dilipa of epic vintage, do not seem to have sound historical basis.

There *does* seem to be some historical basis for accounts which connect the founding of the city with the Tomara Rajputs. Legends about the Tomara kings, particularly about their being the founders of Dilli, are preserved in bardic tradition and are also recounted in certain medieval texts. Abul Fazl states explicitly that the city of Dilli was founded in year 429 of the Vikrama era (i.e. 371–2 AD)[49] by the Tomara king Anangapala. Legends connecting Anangapala with Delhi are recorded in manuscripts maintained by the *bhats*, the traditional genealogists of India. Sir Alexander Cunningham's reports make special mention of the records of Kharg Rai, a Gwalior *bhat* who lived in the time of the seventeenth-century Mughal emperor Shah Jahan. The bardic tradition gives various confused versions of a story of a *raja* (king) of Dilli being defeated by a Shaka king, who in turn was defeated by a king named Vikramaditya. Kharg Rai states that the city of Dilli was deserted for 792 years after Vikramaditya, and was repeopled by the king Bilan De Tomar (who can be identified with the Tomara king Anangapala I). The descendants of this king continued to rule over Dilli until they were defeated and displaced by the Chauhans under Bisal De (who can be identified with Vigraharaja IV). While the earlier part of this narrative does not seem to have any historical basis, the later part connecting the Tomaras with the founding of a city at Delhi and their being displaced by the Chauhans does.

Some of the details recorded in traditional and bardic histories are echoed in inscriptions. A twelfth-century inscription found in a small town named Bijholia in Rajasthan refers to the Chauhan king Vigraharaja as the conqueror of Dhillika. A few other points connected with the history of the city are mentioned in four inscriptions found in the Delhi area. The thirteenth-century Palam

---

[49] Such an early date is obviously impossible to accept.

Baoli inscription (found in a *baoli* or step well in Palam village, some 12 miles south-west of Delhi) records the construction of a step well by Uddhara, a householder of Dhilli. In its third line, it tells of the land of Hariyanaka, which was first enjoyed by the Tomaras, then by the Chauhans, and still later by the Delhi Sultans (whom the inscription refers to as 'Shakas,' going on to enumerate these kings from Muhammad of Ghor down to Balban). The thirteenth line of the inscription is also of interest to us as it refers to the city of Dhilli as being renowned under the name of Yoginipura, giving us another ancient or early medieval name of the city. A thirteenth-century inscription found on a stone tablet at Sonepat near Delhi (the inscription goes by the name of the Delhi Museum Stone Inscription) records the construction of a well in a village named Suvarnaprastha and tell us in its first two lines that Dhillika in the Hariyana country was ruled successively by the Tomaras, Chahamanas (Chauhans), and Shakas. A fourteenth-century inscription found in Sarban village (in New Delhi near Raisina Road) records the building of a well in Saravala village by two merchants, Khetala and Paitala. Four stanzas speak of the past of Dhilli. The account matches that of the Palam Baoli and Delhi Museum Stone inscriptions, except that the term used for the Turks is not 'Shaka' but 'Turushka.' Saravala village is described in the inscription as located in the *pratigana* (administrative division) of Indraprastha. A fourteenth-century stone inscription found at Naraina in west Delhi records the construction of a village well by a person named Sridhara, and refers to a great province named Hariyana, wherein lay the city of Dhilli. It also describes Nadayana (i.e. Naraina) village as being located to the west of Indraprastha. The name of Indraprastha had evidently lived on for almost two-and-a-half thousand years!

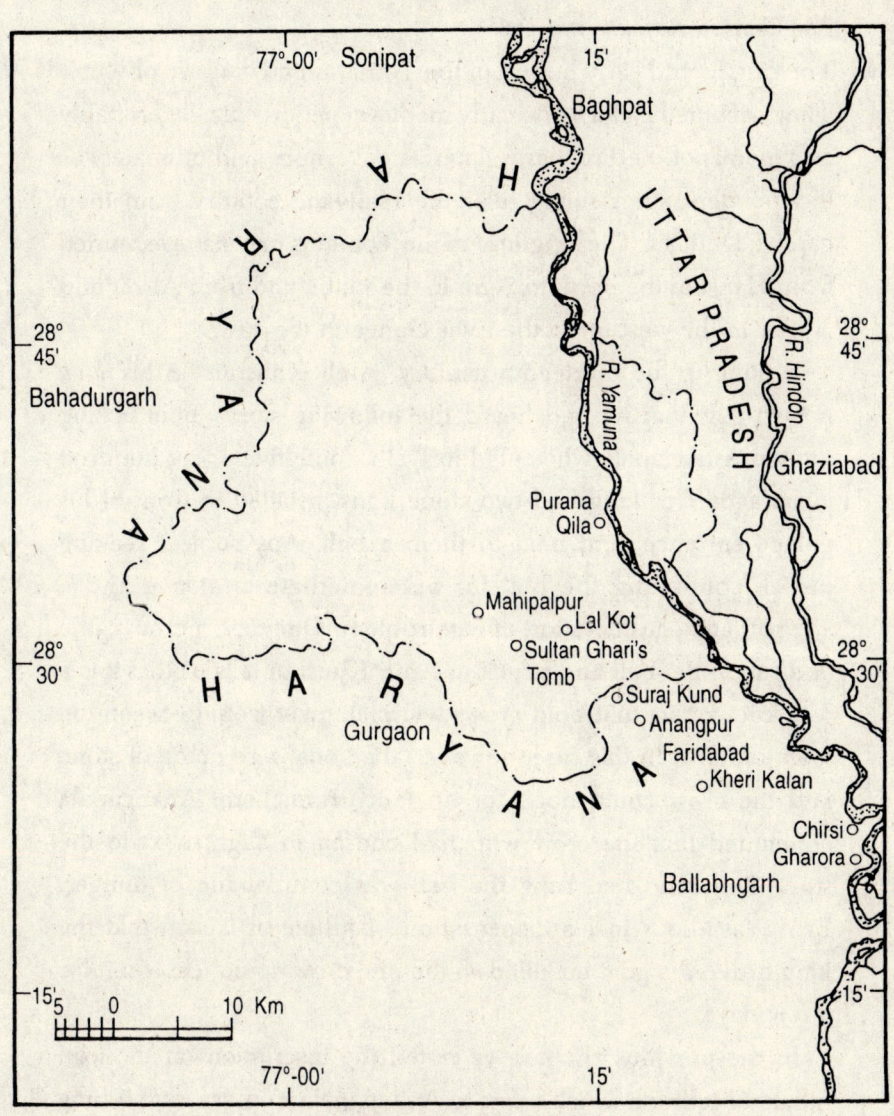

Sites of early medieval finds

The Tomara Rajputs and Delhi

The origins and early history of the Tomaras or Tuars are obscure. They occupied Delhi in the early medieval period, initially probably as generals of the Pratiharas, later as governors, and ultimately as independent kings ruling over the Hariyana country from their capital, Dhillika. The kingdom of the Tomaras may have extended from Hansi in the north to Agra in the south, and from Alwar and Ajmer in the west up to the river Ganga in the east.

Writing in the fourteenth century, Amir Khusrau (in his *Nuh Siphir*) tells that he had heard the following story about a king named Anangapala who ruled in Delhi some five or six hundred years ago: This king had two stone lions installed in front of his palace entrance, and next to them a bell. Any subject seeking justice could ring the bell for an immediate audience and a sympathetic consideration of his problem. One day, a crow came and sat on the bell and struck it. Amir Khusrau tells us that it is a well-known fact that bold crows will pick meat from between the teeth of lions. In this case, however, the lions were made of stone and the crow could hope for no food from them. Anangapala concluded that the crow who had chosen to alight next to the stone lions and had rung the bell was complaining of hunger. Being fastidious in his dispensation of justice, it is said that the king ordered a goat be killed so that the crow could feast on it for a few days.

In the previous chapter we noted the inscription on the iron pillar at Mehrauli which refers to Anangapala Tomara establishing Delhi[50] and the legends which connect him with the city. Remains of the period are found at various places whose names give away

---

[50] Cunningham read the inscription in question as: 'Samvat Dihali 1109 Ang Pal Bahi,' and saw herein a reference to Anangapala 'peopling' Delhi in Samvat 1109 (1052 AD). B.R. Mani reads the inscription a little differently: 'Samvat Kinlli 1109 Angapala badi,' and sees here a reference to the king tightening the nail (i.e.) in that year.

their Tomara connection. Anangpur village (which also goes by the names of Anekpur or Arangpur) in the Badarpur area has been mentioned earlier in this book as an important prehistoric site. On a hillock near the village, there are the ruins of early medieval fortifications and structures. The name of the village connects with it one of the two (or three) Tomara kings named Anangapala. The fortified settlement here may have been founded by Anangapala I or by Anangapala II, the builder of the citadel of Lal Kot. If it was the former, this would date the settlement to around the eighth century, and if the latter, to the eleventh century.

The over 300 m. long stone wall of Anangpur fort runs from the southern slope of the hill northwards to the top and then winds in an elipse around the summit. The fort overlooks a gorge on its southern and western sides. During the rains, this would have filled up with water, forming a sort of moat. Within the fort wall, the traces of a few structures and streets were found near the western gateway. A circular coin (apparently Rajput) was found in this area. On the obverse, it seems to depict Shiva and the Nandi bull, while the reverse bears traces of a now illegible legend. Sherds of a red pottery of medium to coarse fabric were also found. These included fragments of storage jars, lids, cooking vessels, basins, and bowls. A quartzite block with a five-line inscription was discovered standing in the fields of the village. The inscription is written in the Nagari script and has some not-fully-legible numbers on it, probably the date. Another find from the lower area of the hill in the village is a stone sculpture depicting a seated drummer flanking the main figure which is broken. The sculpture seems to belong to the ninth or tenth century. A few surface finds of fragments of glazed pottery from the hill suggest that occupation at the site of Anangpur did not end with the Rajput phase but continued into the Sultunate period.

The stone masonry dam near Anangpur was probably also built
by one of the Anangapalas. Constructed in order to block upstream
rainwater for irrigation purposes, it is about 50 m. wide and 7 m.
high and has sluices for controlling the flow of water. The reservoir
of Suraj Kund (about 3 km. south-east of Tughluqabad) is also
supposed to have been built by a Tomara king—Suraj Pala. This
reservoir is bounded by a semi-circular stepped stone embankment.
Some carved stones found in the area suggest that there may have
been a Sun temple on its western side. Firuz Shah Tughluq effected
some repairs and additions to the reservoir.

Anangapala II was in all likelihood the builder of the tank known
as Anang Tal, about a quarter of a mile north-west of the Qutb
Minar. The tank measures 169′ × 152′ and is 40′ deep. It is dry
now, but medieval sources tell us that during the construction of
Alauddin Khilji's *minar* (the unfinished *minar* situated in the vicinity
of the Qutb Minar), the water for the mortar was brought from
this tank. The Tomara kings are thus associated with the
construction of the earliest known water-works in the Delhi region.

Another place associated with the name of a Tomara king is
the village of Mahipalpur, two miles north-east of the Qutb Minar.
Here again, there is a tank with an embankment, about ¾ x ¼
mile in dimensions. It is supposed to have been built by Firuz
Shah Tughluq.

Lal Kot

The fort of Lal Kot in the Mehrauli was in all likelihood built by
Anangapala II in the middle of the eleventh century. The damaged
ramparts of this early medieval fort have a circumference of almost
3.6 km. and enclose an area of about 763, 875 sq. m. Excavations
carried out here between 1957 and 1961 concentrated mainly on
the fortification walls. One of the interesting discoveries was that

The ruins at Lal Kot
Photograph: Aditya Arya

the original wall had been built of rubble stone to a height of about 8'; over this, there were 30 courses of kiln-burnt bricks. The flight of stairs leading to the wall was similarly made of stone in the lower section and brick in the upper section. This suggests two phases in the building of the fortification wall. We cannot be absolutely sure whether the stonework belongs to the Rajput phase and the brickwork to the Sultanate phase, but this is a possibility. A single coin of the bull-and -horseman type was found during the excavations.

The more recent excavations carried out at Lal Kot under the direction of B.R. Mani between 1991 and 1995 revealed various aspects of the citadel and the Anang Tal, and brought to light a profusion of antiquities.[51] Two cultural phases were identified—

---

[51] Details of the Lal Kot excavations are given in Mani's *Delhi*. This book also has photographs

Period I belonging to the Rajput phase (the mid-11th century to the end of the 12th century), and Period II to the Sultanate phase (the end of the 12th century to the mid-14th century). The first was further divided into three structural phases and the second into four. The pottery of the Rajput period included various kinds of bowls, basins, lids, cooking pots (*handis*), vases, miniature vases, lamps and spouted vessels. In its early phase, the pottery included a plain red ware, sometimes with red slip, and a decorated ware with designs incised, painted, or sometimes stamped on. In the later phase, there was the occasional occurrence of a plain glazed ware with ordinary terracotta core, a black-slipped grey ware and a red ware.

A profusion of beautiful artefacts were discovered in the course of the excavations. Notable finds of the Rajput period included a sculpture of the elephant-headed god Ganesha executed on a small rectangular piece of sandstone. There was also part of a terracotta mould for casting a Jaina *tirthankara* figure flanked by two attendants.[52] Among the copper coins, one had the word 'Devi' on the obverse and a crude representation of a fire altar on the reverse. Four others were of the horseman-and-bull type. The finds included a copper ring; an iron arrow-head; beads made of terracotta, glass, and semi-precious stones; pieces of bangles made of glass, ivory, and bone; finger rings of copper and semi-precious stones like quartz and lapis lazuli; and animal figurines. Many stone sculptures of Period I were found in Period II levels and on the surface of the site—*tirthankaras*, various deities, a Nandi bull, and a lion's head were some of the pieces recovered.[53]

Due to the fact that there were a large number of Sultanate

---

of many of the artefacts.

[52] The saints of the Jainas are known as *tirthankaras*.

[53] Artefacts of one archaeological phase find their way into other strata when the site is

period structures at Lal Kot, very little is known about the earlier Rajput ones. One of the interesting aspects of the buildings of the second period was the use of architectural or sculptural fragments of the first. These included a stone *varaha* (boar) figure, and two stone *amalakas* (knotched ring stones). A single potsherd bearing an inscription in fourth century Brahmi letters indicated the possibility that Lal Kot may have an earlier history, while two PGW sherds found at Sultanate levels suggested that there may be a proto-historic site nearby.

The walls, platforms, and steps of the Anang Tal were identified during the excavations. The tank was oblong in plan. The main approach seems to have been down a flight of steps leading to it on the southern side. Mason marks found on the large, semi-dressed stone blocks used in constructing the tank include symbols such as the *svastika*, trident, circle divided into four parts, drum, numerals, letters, scorpion, and bow-and-arrow.

The sculptural fragments found during the Lal Kot excavations and the myriad of reassembled sculptural and pillar fragments in the courtyard of the Qutb Jami Masjid strongly suggest that there was a large temple complex in this area during the Rajput period. The Anang Tal may have been associated with this temple complex.

The Chauhans and Qila Rai Pithora

The Tomaras were eventually displaced by another Rajput clan, the Chauhans or the Chahamanas. Delhi was captured from the Tomaras by the Chauhan king Vigraharaja IV (the Visala Deva of the traditional bardic histories) in the middle of the twelfth century AD. The Tomaras may have retained some

---

disturbed. That is why ancient pottery (and other) remains can sometimes be spotted on the *surface* of a site.

of their domain, but had to accept a position of subordination.
We have already noted the three inscriptions of Vigraharaja IV
on the Delhi–Topra pillar, one of which boasts of his conquests
from the Himalayas to the Vindhyas. Prithviraja III, popularly
known as Rai Pithora, was one of Vigraharaja's nephews. Various
bardic accounts, including the biographical epic, the *Prithviraja
Raso* composed by Chand Bardai, tell us of Prithviraja's many
battles, including his victory over Muhammad of Ghor in the first
battle of Tarain (1191) and his subsequent defeat in the second
encounter on the same battlefield (1192). A section of the *Prithviraja
Raso* tells the story of the love story of Prithviraja and Samyogita,
the daughter of the king of Kanauj, and of how the Rajput hero
abducted and later married the lady concerned.[54]

Minhaj us Siraj's account of the defeat of Prithviraja in the second
battle of Tarain narrates that the Rajput king, who was riding an
elephant, dismounted and fled on horse-back, only to be captured
and killed in the vicinity of Sirsuti. Abul Fazl, on the other hand,
gives a different story. He states that he had heard that after his
defeat at Tarain, Prithviraja was taken prisoner and carried to
Ghazni by Muhammad of Ghor. The devoted bard Chand Bardai
entered the Sultan's service, gained his favour and also access to
his former master. Chand proposed that he should praise the
Rajput's skill in archery to the Sultan, who would then want to see
it for himself. The plan worked. Prithviraja pierced Muhammad
of Ghor with an arrow, whereupon the royal retainers fell on
Prithviraja and Chand, cutting them to pieces. Thus, according to
this alternative account, ended the life of the legendary Rajput
king.

Sir Syed Ahmad Khan was of the opinion that the first storey of

---

[54] One of the objections raised by certain scholars is that this incident couldn't have really
happened because it is just too romantic to be true. This seems to be more a comment

the Qutb Minar was a 'Hindu monument,' built during the time of Prithviraja Chauhan, and that the Turks added the subsequent storeys.[55] This theory was convincingly refuted by Alexander Cunningham. A two-word inscription on the ninth course of the jamb of the main entrance door of the Qutb Minar does refer to a king named Prithvi who may be identified with one of the Prithvirajas of the Chauhan dynasty. But this inscribed slab seems to have originally belonged to some other structure.

More monumental evidence of Chauhan rule over Delhi is to be found in the ruins of Qila Rai Pithora, the citadel built by Prithviraja Chauhan, which lies to the north and east of Ananga-pala's Lal Kot. Qila Rai Pithora is much larger that Lal Kot (which forms its south-western part). Exactly *how* large it is difficult to say because the entire circuit of the fortifications is not traceable. The walls, 5–6 m. thick and 18 m. high at places, were interrupted by several gates, only a few of which survive. In the course of the 1957–8 excavations, a section of a wall of Qila Rai Pithora was exposed. Several well-laid structures, including an oven and floors of houses were revealed.

After the defeat of Prithviraja Chauhan, Qila Rai Pithora was occupied by the victorious Turks. The Sultans of Delhi continued to rule from here till the early fourteenth century, when Alauddin Khalji built a new capital city in Delhi at Siri.

---

on the dull life-style of historians rather than a serious critique of the historicity of the incident.

[55] Sir Syed Ahmad Khan is best known as a socio-religious reformer of the nineteenth-century. He was also, however, the author of a classic work which catalogued and described the monuments of Delhi. His *Asar-al-Sanadid* (in the Urdu language) was first published in 1846; the second edition appeared in 1854. The text was accompanied by 130 free-hand sketches by Mirza Shah Rukh Beg, printed by wood-cuts, and with copies of many inscriptions. A French translation of the work appeared in the mid-nineteenth-century. For what is supposed to be an English rendering of Sir Syed's work, *see* R. Nath's *Monuments of Delhi: Historical Study* (New Delhi, 1979). This is, however, a severely abridged version of the Urdu original.

Back to the Purana Qila

Remains of the Rajput period at the Purana Qila included structures
made of reused bricks. One of the houses showed alternate courses
of baked and mud bricks. There were mud-floors with hearths in
some houses. The most impressive structure of the period was a
rubble fortification wall. Unlike Lal Kot and Qila Rai Pithora,
these fortifications are not connected with the name of any
particular king; nor do we know the relationship between this site
and the other two. Finds at Rajput levels at the Purana Qila included
coins of the bull and horse-man type, crude terracotta figurines,
terracotta beads, a pot-sherd with a damaged Nagari inscription,
and ornate moulded bricks.[56] The pottery included mainly red

Purana Qila: terracottas of the Rajput period
Courtesy: Archaeological Survey of India

[56] According to Mani, the Purana Qila terracottas that have been assigned to the Rajput

and black wares, sometimes decorated with simple painted, stamped, or incised designs, a knuckle design being common on the rims of vases. The 1970–1 excavations identified five structural phases of the Rajput period, some showing floors with ovens. Structures made of brick and rubble were also discovered. The fortification wall was found to be badly damaged on the east. Pieces of coral and crystal, a carnelian bead, high-necked jars resembling *surahis*, shallow dishes, a few fragments of carved stone tablets, and a small stone figure of Vishnu were also discovered. An interesting find was a jug containing bells, *ghunghroos* (anklets with bells), and various other objects of copper.

Vestiges of early medieval temples

No traces of structures of ancient or early medieval temples can be seen in or around Delhi today. A large number of sculptural remains have, however, been found at various places, and some of them may have been associated with temples in this area. An early thirteenth century four-armed stone image of Vishnu, found in the Qutb area, is now displayed in the National Museum. A small image of a four-armed Vishnu was reported at Chirsi village in the Faridabad district. Shiva *lingas* and sculptural remains were found at Kheri Kalan in Faridabad. A sculptural piece depicting Jaina *tirthankaras* and fragments of what may have been railings of a shrine have been found at Gharora village (also in Faridabad), suggesting that there must have been a Jaina temple close by. There are frequent references to the importance of Yoginipura and Dhilli in Jaina texts. Several Jaina (as also Hindu) sculptured pillar fragments were reused in the construction of the Jami Masjid in the Qutb complex. An inscription of Qutb-ud-din Aibak over

period actually belong to the early Sultanate period. This is because similar terracottas were found at Lal Kot at levels that definitely belonged to the Sultanate period.

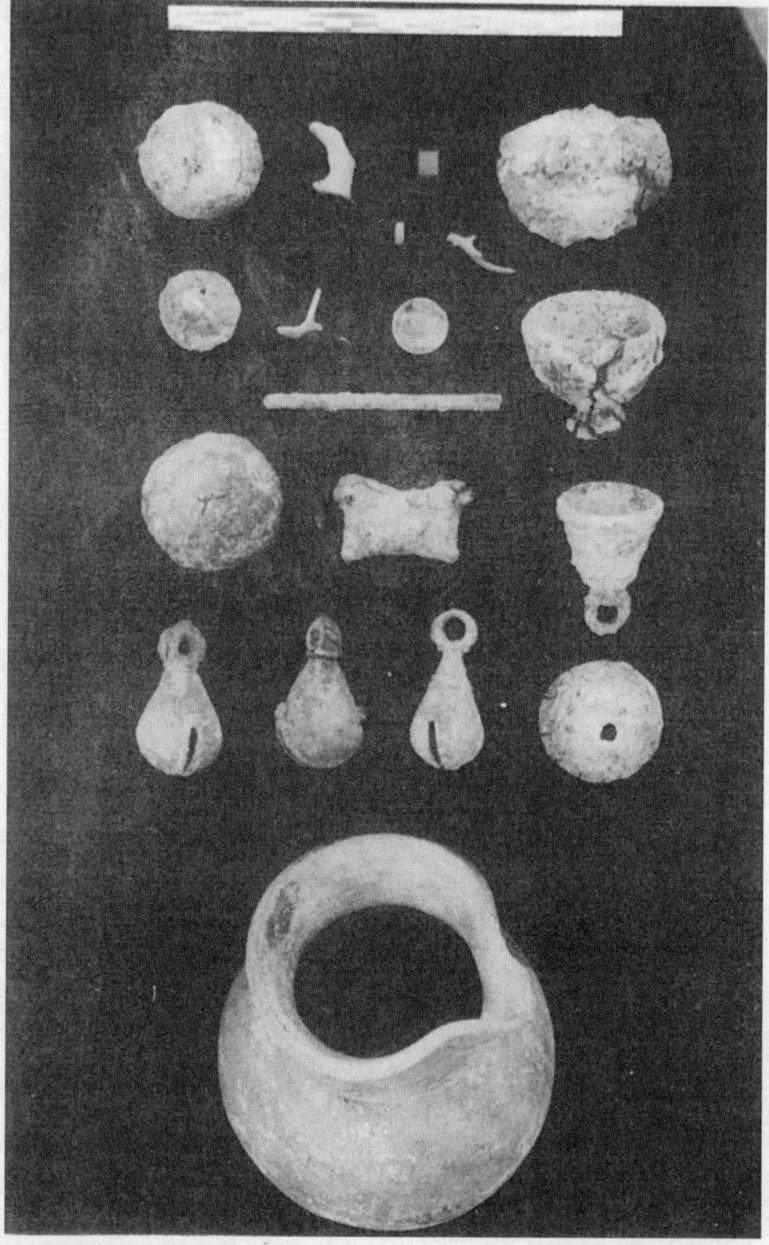

Purana Qila: earthen pot with bells and other items; Rajput period
Courtesy: Archaeological Survey of India

Vishnu image; 13th century
Courtesy: National Museum

the eastern entrance of the Jami Masjid (or the Quwwat-ul-Islam mosque, as it is referred to today) states that it was built from the ruins of twenty-seven temples. Cunningham suggested that the mosque was originally the site of a Hindu temple and that the lower part of the surrounding walls of the raised terrace on which the mosque stands was in fact the original platform of this temple. He identified the tall single-shaft pillars behind the arch as parts of the original shrine. The rest of the pillars in the colonnades in the courtyard of the mosque were recyled and reassembled parts of pillars from this and other temples that existed in the vicinity.

Yoginipura as the name of an ancient or early medieval settlement in the Delhi area may have been connected with a Yogini temple which no longer survives.[57] There is a shrine known as the Jogmaya temple near Mehrauli, associated with the Devi who, assuming the form of an infant, took the place of the baby Krishna in the prison where he was born. According to the legend Kansa, the king of Mathura tried to kill her, but she disappeared into the sky. The Jogmaya temple was built in the early nineteenth century, but it may be a descendant of a much older Devi shrine.[58] As for Mehrauli, if the name was derived from 'Mihirapuri,' (*mihira* means the sun) this may indicate that it had some connection with sun-worship or a sun-temple in earlier times.

About 8 km. south-west of the Qutb Minar is the thirteenth-century tomb of Sultan Ghari, the eldest son of the Mamluk Sultan Iltutmish. It is the oldest known monumental tomb of the Sultanate period. Here, sculpted sandstone lintels and a railing pillar apparently belonging to the seventh/eighth century, were found

---

[57] The *yoginis* are fearsome, ghoulish beings.

[58] It should be mentioned that apart from a certain phonetic similarity between their names, the Yognis and the goddess Jogmaya are quite different in character. Of course it is possible that the Jogmaya temple was built at the site where a Yogini temple once stood, but there is no proof for this.

The Chirsi Vishnu
Photograph: N. Lahiri

Tirthankara image at Gharora
Photograph: N. Lahiri

embedded in the roof concrete of the tomb. A marble *yoni-patta* (base slab for a Shiva *linga*) was found reused in the floor of the prayer chamber of the tomb. Once again, as in the case of the Ashokan columns and the Gupta iron pillar, we see how remains of an earlier period were appropriated by a later age.

With this comment on the mingling of the ages, we come to the end of *this* story of Delhi's ancient past. A few things remain to be said. The first is that a history of a place based entirely on references in written texts and the evidence of imposing monuments can only be a partial history. There is, therefore, an urgent need to carefully and meticulously survey and document details of sites, structures, surface finds, and to record local memories and traditions reflected in people's oral testimony. Secondly, many of the sites and relics of Delhi's ancient past are fast disappearing due to neglect or various activities inevitably associated with modern times. There is also, therefore, an urgent need to protect and preserve. This is important because when we lose the signs of our past we lose the past itself.

Glossary

Acheulian: an advanced technique of making hand-axes

artefact: any object made or altered by human hands

ashvamedha: the 'horse sacrifice;' a complex ancient Indian ritual, signifying a claim to political paramountcy

bhats: the traditional genealogists of India

brahmi: an ancient Indian script

cultural sequence: the order of cultural levels at a site

culture: in its narrowest archaeological sense a recurring assemblage of material traits; in its broader sense patterns of learned behaviour that comprise the way of life of a community

doab: the land between the Ganga and Yamuna

factory site: a site where tools were made

grama-sthana: village shrine

hand-axe: a kind of stone tool with a broad butt-end and tapering sides; usually worked on both sides

holocene: the geological era that began about 10, 000 years ago and that continues into our own time

hominids: man-like species

Janamejaya: the son of king Parikshit; great-grand-son of Arjuna; performer of the great snake-sacrifice

in situ: in its original place

iron slag: the waste product of iron smelting

khera: a local word for 'mound' prevalent in the Delhi area

Late Harappan: the late, post-urban phase of the Harappan culture

linga: the phallus; an emblem of the god Shiva, symbolizing his virility and
   procreative potential

Magadha: a kingdom that arose in the early historical period in south-east
   Bihar

mesolithic: stone age cultures of post-pleistocene times with an economy that
   revolved mainly around hunting and gathering and a tool-kit that included
   microliths

microliths: tiny stone tools

mukha-linga: a stone phallic emblem of the god Shiva with his face carved on it

murti: religious icon

neolithic: a phase of the stone age which saw the beginnings of food-production
   based on animal and plant domestication, and certain new techniques of
   polishing, pecking and grinding stone tools

Northern Black Polished Ware (NBPW): a pottery type the use of which can be
   placed roughly between 600 B.C. to 100 B.C.

Painted Grey Ware (PGW): a pottery type which was in use in certain parts of
   India roughly between 1000 B.C. to 500 B.C..

palaeo-channels: remnants of old courses of a river

palaeolithic: a phase of the stone age that is associated with the pleistocene
   geological era, a hunting-gathering economy, and certain characteristic stone
   tools.

Parikshit: son of Abhimanyu; grand-son of Arjuna; he became king after the
   Mahabharata war; died due to a snake-bite

pleistocene: the geological era that preceded the holocene

rishi: sage

sangha: monastic order

sealing: clay impression of a seal

site: a place where artefacts are found

slip: coating on pottery

tapasya: religious austerities

tirthankara: a Jaina saint

Select Bibliography

Babu, B.S.R. Mandoli, 'A Late Harappan Settlement in Delhi,' in C. Margabandhu, and K.S. Ramachandran, (eds), *Spectrum of Indian Culture* (Professor S.B. Deo Felicitation volume), Delhi, 1996, pp. 98–104.

——, 'Excavations at Bhorgarh,' in *Puratattva*, No. 25 (1994–5), pp. 88–93.

Chakrabarti. Dilip K. and N. Lahiri, 'A Preliminary Report on the Stone Age of the Union Territory of Delhi and Haryana', in *Man and Environment*, XI (1987), pp. 109–16.

Cunningham, Alexander, *Archaeological Survey of India: Four Reports Made during the Years 1862–63–64–65*, vol. 1(1871); reprint edn., Delhi, Varanasi, 1972.

——, *Annual Report of the Archaeological Survey of India*, IV vols IV (1871–2); V (1872–3); XIV (1878–9).

The Delhi Ridge Forest: Decline and Conservation. Kalpavriksh. New Delhi. 1991.

Elliot, H.M. and J. Dowson, *The History of India as told by Its Own Historians: Tarikh-i Firoz Shahi of Shams-i Siraj Afif*, repr. Calcutta, 1953.

Frykenberg, R.E. (ed.), *Delhi Through the Ages: Essays in Urban History, Culture and Society*, Delhi, 1986.

Gazetteer of the Delhi District, 1883–4, reprinted as *A Gazetteer of Delhi (1883–4).* Gurgaon, 1988.

Gazetteer of the Delhi District, Delhi, 1912.

Gazetteer of India: Delhi Gazetteer, Delhi, 1976.

Grover, A.K. and P.L. Bakliwal, 'River Migration and the Floods—A Study of Yamuna River through Remote Sensing.' *Man and Environment*, 9 (1985), pp. 151–3.

Hasan, Maulavi Zafar, *Monuments of Delhi: Lasting Splendour of the Great Mughals and Others*. J.A. Page et. al. (eds), Introduction by R.C. Agrawal. 3 vols first published, 1916. Reprint edn., New Delhi, 1997.

Hultzsch, E. (ed.), *Corpus Inscriptionum Indicarnum,* vol. 1, Delhi, 1925.

Indian Archaeology–A Review, 1954–5, 1969–70, 1970–1.

Joshi, M.C. and B.M. Pande. 'A Newly-discovered Inscription of Asoka at Bahapur, Delhi', *Journal of the Royal Asiatic Society of Great Britain and Ireland,* 1967.

Kaul, H.K. *Historic Delhi: An Anthology.* Delhi.1985. (1996 paperback edn.).

Lahiri, Nayanjot, Upinder Singh, and Tarika Uberoi, 'Preliminary Field Report on the Archaeology of Faridabad,' in *Man and Environment,* XXI (1996), pp. 32–57.

Maheshwari, J.K., *The Flora of Delhi*, New Delhi: Council of Scientific and Industrial Research, 1963.

Mani, B.R., *Delhi: Threshold of the Orient (Studies in Archaeological Investigations),* New Delhi, 1997.

—— 'Excavations at Lal Kot 1991–2 and Further Explorations in Delhi,' *Puratattva*, No. 22 (1991–2). pp. 75–87.

—— 'Earliest Remains of Delhi Sultanate: New Evidence from Excavations at Lal Kot 1991–3', in C. Margabandhu and K.S. Ramachandran, (eds), *Spectrum of Indian Culture* (Professor S.B. Deo Felicitation volume). Delhi, 1996. pp. 250–4.

Mani, B.R. and I.D. Dwivedi, 'Anangpur Fort: The Earliest Tomar Settlement near Delhi,' in *Puratattva,* No. 24 (1993–4). pp. 41–3.

Nath, R., *Monuments of Delhi: Historical Study*, New Delhi, Indian Institute of Islamic Studies, 1979.

Raychaudhuri, Hemachandra, *Political History of Ancient India,* reprint edn, Delhi, 1996.

Sharma, Y.D., *Delhi and Its Neighbourhood,* New Delhi, Archaeological Survey, 1990.

Sharma, A.K., *Prehistoric Delhi and Its Neighbourhood,* New Delhi, 1993.

Sircar, D.C., 'New Delhi Inscription of Asoka', *Epigraphia Indica,* vol. 38. 1969–70, pp. 1–4.

Stephen, Carr, *The Archaeology and Monumental Remains of Delhi,* first edn.,

1876. Reprint edn., New Delhi.

van Buitenan, J.A.B. (trans. and ed.), *The Mahabharata*, Chicago, vol. 1, 1973, vol. 2, 1975.

Index

Kurukshetra 29, 39

Lal Kot 94-97
Late Harappan sites 22-27

Magadha 47-48
Mahabharata 1, 28-33, 39-42
Mahipalpur 94
Malavas 64
Mandoli 23-25, 43, 66, 71-73, 84
Maukharis 86
Mauryas 48, 50, 63

Nachauli 26-27, 72-73
Naraina stone inscription 90
Nigambodh 38
Nili Chhatri temple 11, 38
Northern Black Polished Ware
   (NBP) pottery/sites 48-50

Painted Grey Ware (PGW)
   pottery/sites 33-34, 36-37, 39-40,
   42-45, 97
Palm Baoli inscription 89-90
Parsaun 11
Pratiharas 86-87
Prinsep, James 52 and n., 77-78
Prithviraja Chauhan 98

Prithviraja Raso 82
Ptolemy 65-66
Purana Qila 33-39, 50, 66, 83-84,
   87, 100-1
Pushyabhutis 86-87

Qila Rai Pithora 99
Qutb complex 76-77, 97, 101, 104

Rajputs 88 ff.
Ridge 7-8

Sarban stone inscription 90
Shungas 63
Sihi 40, 43
stone age sites 14-15
stone age tools 18-20
Sultan Ghari's tomb 104-5
Suraj Kund 94

Tilpat 39-40, 42-43, 73
Tomaras 81, 88-90, 92-97

Yamuna 8-12
Yashovarman 86-87
Yaudheyas 64-65
Yoginipura 90, 101, 104